STREET PHOTOG

A Photographic
Survival Manual

by Peter J. Nebergall

Photos by the Author

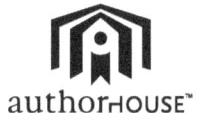

author**HOUSE**™

1663 LIBERTY DRIVE, SUITE 200
BLOOMINGTON, INDIANA 47403
(800) 839-8640
WWW.AUTHORHOUSE.COM

First published by AuthorHouse 04/07/05

ISBN: 1-4208-3765-6 (sc)

Printed in the United States of America
Bloomington, Indiana

This book is printed on acid-free paper.

For Lester Wilson, who taught a kid what he knew. Thanks.

PJN 11/03

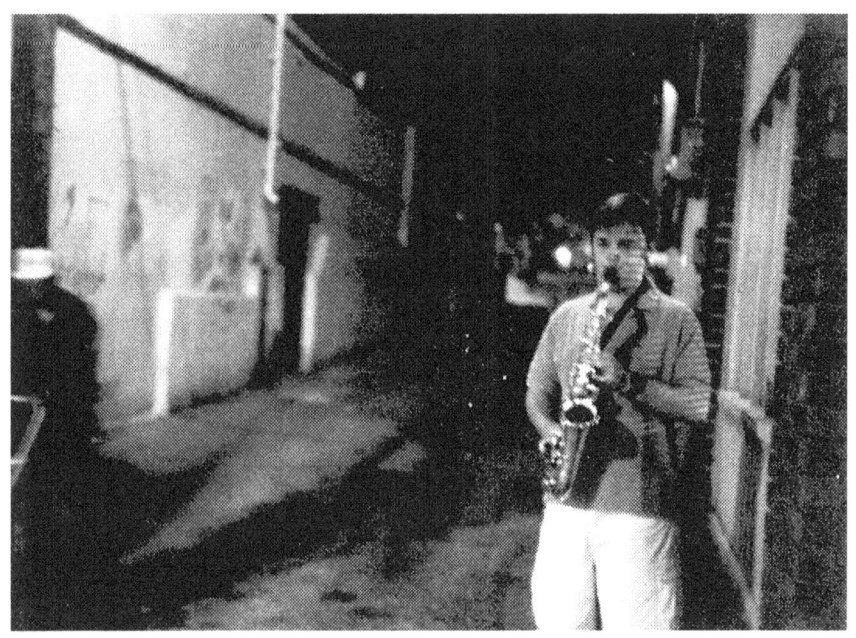

Table of Contents

INTRODUCTION I

EQUIPMENT 3

THE SNAPSHOT.. 9

LEARNING COMPOSITION.. I3

PEOPLE PICTURES... I7

THINKING ABOUT PORTRAITURE 23

PHOTOGRAPHY AND THE LAW.. 29

USING DIGITAL.. 33

ABOUT "SHARPNESS"... 37

SEEING AND MEANING.. 4I

THINKING ABOUT THE ZONE SYSTEM 45

THINGS THAT MOVE... 49

WILDLIFE PHOTOGRAPHY 53

ROCK AND ROLL 57

AERIAL... 6I

SKIN ART 63

WAR PHOTOGRAPHY 69

SMALL OBJECTS.. 73

WEDDING PHOTOGRAPHY 77

VISUAL ANTHROPOLOGY 8I

PHOTOGRAPHY AND YOUR CHILD................................ 85

EDITING... 87

ARCHIVAL STORAGE...91

YOUR PORTFOLIO 95

PHOTOGRAPHY AS A BUSINESS 99

A PHOTOGRAPHER'S SOCIAL SKILLS.. 103

LITTLE STORIES SECTION 105
    A KID PHOTOGRAPHER GETS LUCKY.............................. 105
    MY STRANGEST ASSIGNMENT.. 109
    READING PICTURES: A CASE STUDY 111
    THE ASPIRING JOURNALIST.. 113
IN CONCLUSION 115

APPENDIX: Reading List.. 121

INTRODUCTION

Photography is like jazz -- there's a whole lot of ways to play it. Just as there are good, competent, creative jazzmen, masters of their art -- who have nothing in common with each other, and know it, there are master photographers whose work leaves each other cold -- and that's *all right*. That's the world.

No master, no style, no guru has valid claim to superiority. There is no "better way," no "ultimate." What moves you, as a *creator*? What moves you, as an *observer*? What *works*?

Talk to any teacher; what you will learn is not THE way, but HIS way. Of course all a teacher can impart is *his own wisdom* -- but too many would have you believe theirs is *the only valid path*. It *ain't*. *Its* **your own horn** *you're learnin' how to blow* -- not **his**.

Walk with me. I've been taking pictures since age eight, and making money doing it since I was 13 years old. In this book I'll show you *my* way, and how I learned to do it. It might be right for you, or not. That's your business. The best way to learn photography, or anything, really, is to explore a lot of different paths -- and in these pages I'll show you mine.

EQUIPMENT

Listen to the admen -- everything is "ultimate," every competing product represents an evolutionary pinnacle -- and if you just buy *This* one (not *That* one!), you're set for life -- success is guaranteed. Right?

Maybe you shouldn't listen to the admen.....

Reality check -- life's not like that. Neither is photography. When I was first learning how to play guitar, I was convinced that if I had one like my teacher's, I'd sound *so much better*. Then one day my teacher picked up mine -- and demolished that idea, with a beautiful string of chords and runs. "It's how you play it," he said.

Supplying rich dilettante yuppies with the latest trendy do-everything gadgets is a billion-dollar industry. Cameras are part of it, just like high-fashion running shoes. But you don't need Nikes to run fast and win, and you don't need the latest grand ultimate autofocus motordrive ergonomic plastic digital superzoom computer-enhanced whatever, to take good pictures. But yes, there's some very rich guys getting richer by convincing you that you *do*...

What do *you* need? Which kind of equipment is right for you? Depends on what you want, or *need*, to do. A photo student needs something that will help, perhaps even *force*, him/her to learn. A news photographer needs reliability and versatility. A sports photographer, or a wildlife photographer, needs speed, quick handling, and ease with long lenses. A portrait photographer

3

generally needs a bigger machine, with lots of features that let him/her manipulate the image. A museum photographer, or archaeological photographer, needs steadiness, sharpness, and "macro" (very close focus) capabilities. An art photographer needs manual control over all features, and a street photog (like yours truly) needs equipment that is small, quick, unobtrusive, and unintimidating.

Compare all this to the popular yuppie "point and shoot." That camera is optimized for the ignorant. Focus? It does it for you. Settings? It does it for you. You hand over all creative control to the on-board computer -- and go veg out -- smoke some dope or something. For the uncommitted, the P&S is the logical successor to the old "box camera." "You push the button; we do the rest," Kodak used to say, and that's about the size of it. You can't learn anything with a P&S, except the price of film, processing, and batteries.

The P&S has a few more downsides, too. One of them is reliability. Point and shoot machines are enormously complex, and break often. They're for yuppies, who might shoot eight rolls of film in a year -- and then in a few years trade the camera in for a more "with it" model, or else lose interest, and go do something else. That's their niche.

The average professional shoots more film in a week -- perhaps in a day. No P&S is reliable enough. The P&S has a fixed lens (you can't interchange it), and the "zoom" lenses on some of the pricier P&S cameras are of insufficient range, insufficient speed (too small maximum F-stop), and insufficient close-focus ability. You pay a lot for a high-end P&S -- they are very trendy -- but you really don't get a lot for your money.

The trick is to find something to learn with, without paying so much for it that you feel obligated to keep it. A good learner's camera may well be completely wrong for the photographic niche you eventually find.

What's a good learner's camera? Since the average student is somewhere just this side of broke, *cheapness* is an important consideration. In this day and age, that means the *used camera store*. They're not trendy, used cameras, they don't advertise your father's Wall Street success, but then *whadd'ya want?* They work, just as well or better than the new ones, and you can learn on them.

What's good? Old 35mm SLR (single lens reflex) cameras, with or without light meters inside them, are a good choice for the student. Many used models either take currently available interchangeable lenses, or else (lucky you!) an obsolete lensmount, and boxes full of them, with cheap pricetags, and *your name* on them, are waiting in the back room. You can learn, properly, with a used 35mm SLR, and you won't need a mortgage.

Nikon, for years a dominant supplier of top professional cameras, asked its researchers how many exposures a pro might put through his 35mm camera in a lifetime. *How long should a camera last?* It seemed most cameras were good for maybe 10,000 exposures -- and Nikon built its "F" series to last *50,000 exposures.* Old Nikon F cameras, unless utterly beat to death, will probably outlast *any* of the current "plastic fantastic" types. They're a great starter choice.

Other student choices might include the 6x6cm TLR (twin lens reflex) camera -- great for learning (I did) but harder to find film and processing -- and the 35mm rangefinder camera (once "obsolescent," but now undergoing a renaissance, as eyes age and folks rediscover how fast and convenient the rangefinder can be, especially in low light). Other machines, like the 6x6cm SLR, the 6x7cm rangefinder, and the "645" or "ideal format" cameras, are too expensive, too specialized, niche-market cameras for established professionals. You may decide you need one, eventually.

What do I use? I have a lot of cameras -- probably far too many. I buy cameras when I'm depressed, and for some years now, life's been depressing. But I have a bunch of old Nikons, rock-solid 35mm SLR machines built for the news professionals of the 1960s and 1970s. Nikons keep running -- they're built that way -- and old "Fs" in "user" condition are cheaper than your point and shoot. They'll last longer too, and thousands of lenses fit them.

I've used Asahi/Honeywell Pentaxes, of the screw-mount variety. They're lighter and smaller than the Nikons, with great lenses, and cheap -- but for truly heavy use they're a little less than 100% reliable. *You can break a Pentax.*

5

I've used old Exaktas, made in Dresden, East Germany. They're classy, they're weird-looking, and there's a wonderful collection of great lenses available to put on them, from Zeiss, Schneider, Schacht, Meyer, Steinheil, and Angenieux -- cheap. The Exakta was always an "artist's camera," not rugged enough for the newsie. It provided (still does) lots of control, but wasn't meant for the newsroom, or the battlefield. Its a great learner's machine, provide you find one in good condition, one that doesn't have its shutter curtains dried out (a too-common failing on old *Ossi* (East German) cameras.) I'm sure I'm not the only one who's had an Exakta rebuilt. I have 6 of them.

I've used 6x6 TLR cameras, from Yashica and Rollei. as I said, they're limited, but they force you to learn. Pricing runs the gamut -- rich collectors want the Rolleiflexes -- but an old Yashica "A," or "D," or even their Cadillac, the "Mat-124G," can teach you a lot, for a little. *I have a lot of other machines, but I wouldn't advocate trying to learn on them...*

Lenses? The marketeers think the 50mm "normal" lens (for 35mm SLR or rangefinder) is *passe*. They're wrong. They'd sell you a "short zoom" instead, pushing "convenience" instead of sharpness, reliability, close focus, or low-light capability. Don't try to learn with one. Get the "normal." When you're ready, when you've mastered the basics, *then* worry about telephotos and wide-angle lenses.

Do you need a light meter? Yes. Some cameras have meters in them, either telling you, with needles and lights, how to set F-stop and shutter, or else they set the camera for you ("automatic exposure," or "program.") And the "program" cameras that offer "manual override" (as if it were a condescending favor!) are always a far-bigger pain in the butt to use manually than are the old manual machines they replaced. Ah, progress...

I have a big hand-held light meter, a *Luna-Lux* from Gossen, and, although it does not directly couple with any camera, it is highly accurate, more so than the miniaturized meters inside most cameras. Thus it provides a good check of a camera's inboard metering system (as well as a meter for some of my older cameras that never had one.)

I have nothing autofocus. I don't need it. Like P&S cameras, autofocus passes creative control to the computer. Why bother? And, if the camera has an available "manual override," it'll always be slower and more fiddly than using a manual focus camera. As autofocus makes the camera bigger, more complex, and more fragile (as well as *more expensive!*), leave it.

What about zoom lenses? Are they "universal?" No. The popular "35-135" size is bigger and heavier than a 135mm, and the "35-300" size is bigger, heavier, and more ostentatious than a 300mm telephoto. For me, one of the attractions of shorter focal lengths is their unobtrusiveness. Another is their light weight. I certainly would not want to lug a big long lens around all day unless I absolutely had to! And, zoom lenses are **never as sharp** as their "standard" equivalents. You may not notice it, but in low light, working wide open, you'll see the relative unsharpness -- or your customers will.

Do I *have* any zoom lenses? Yes -- but they're for my sports cameras, where speed is critical, or for my "car cameras," where the issue is convenience. My serious 35mm cameras mount 35mm, 50mm, and 90mm standard lenses. **I suggest you do the same**.

We'll talk more about equipment as we go; these are just the basics.

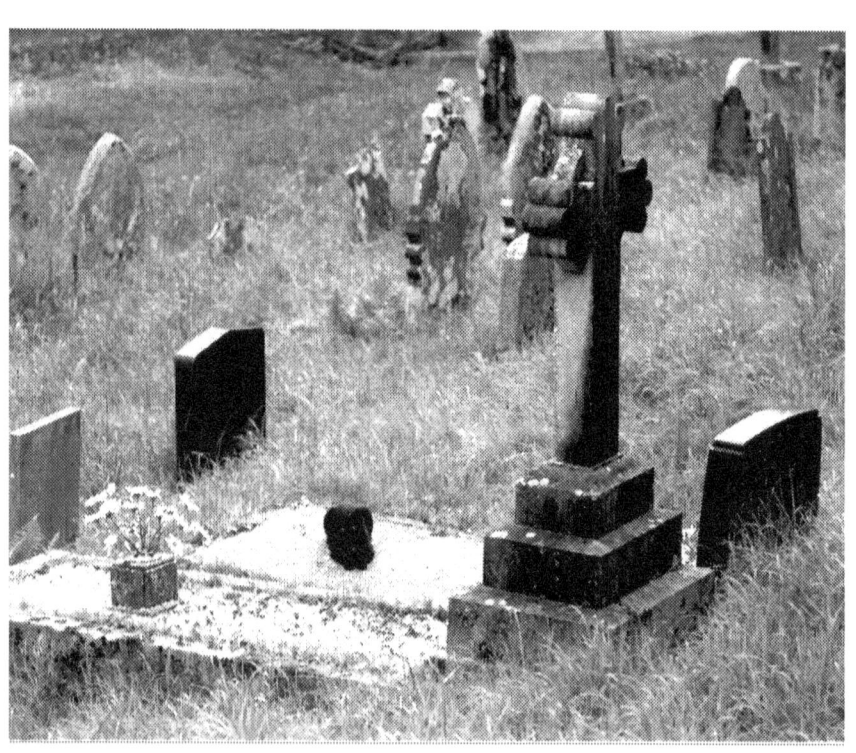

THE SNAPSHOT

What's a "snapshot?" How's it different from an "art" photo, or from a piece of photojournalism? Do "professionals" take "snapshots?"

The differences are two: **Planning and purpose**. "Snapshooting" is a hunter's word -- *it means to whip the gun up and fire, without taking careful aim.* The photographic "snapshot" is the product of unstructured impulse, like a spoiled rich kid dashing through the candy store: *I want THAT!* Why? Who cares?

Long ago, writing for academics, I suggested they put some time into pre-planning their photos. "You can't take a picture of everything," I told them; "You'll run out of money." I suggested to these researchers (archaeology and anthropology students) they take steps to make sure the content of their photos paralleled the direction of their research. Now academic photography is pretty dry -- and those folks really do need to plan, because the point is *to write a paper about something. They need their pictures to belong in that paper.* But we can learn from them.

I divide my photography into "assignment" and "incidental" collections. I always carry a camera, and the "incidentals" are the odd items, quick portraits, and various strangeness I capture because I'm there when it happens. You can't plan for these pictures; you have to be ready for them. *You can't say "hold it," either, as in this day and age that's what the man with the gun says....*

That's "incidental." Anything goes.

My other work is planned. If I'm going to do some horses, I won't be too concerned by flowers, butterflies, or pretty sunsets. And, I'll bother to learn what my customers want -- because they will have specific things they want to see in the photos they buy from me. A major difference between commercial photography (what I do) and "Art" photography is that *I'm* not being paid to be contemplative, "expressive," or in any way self-indulgent. My customers have a good idea *what they want* -- and I'm paid to *deliver what they want* -- to them. The standards for content are set by the customer -- not by the photographer. I'm a contractor -- and the customer wrote the contract -- so I'd better read the fine print.

A lot of magazines and graphics companies (best example *Hallmark*) buy photos -- and these people have pretty explicit lists of what they want and don't want. Find these lists on the web, at these corporations, or in publications like *Photographer's Market*.

Now, just by accident, you might come up with a snapshot that happens to fill a specific niche -- and it might sell. Accidents do happen. That's a snapshot. But, what if, instead, you *know* what the greeting card companies are looking for (*'cuz you looked*, and *asked*) and you have three or four buyers on file who told you "I'll buy one of *those* if you get me a good one?"

When I go "prospecting," even just "incidental" work, I already know what I want, for the various groups that buy from me. For my book projects, I already know the themes, and I'll go for new images that fit those themes. That's preparation. It makes you money.

Does this mean I will categorically reject a good picture that's not in the theme I'm working at the moment? Of course not. It means only that I won't distract myself from the job at hand by seeking "off the path" images -- but if one sits down in front of me, or above me, I'll get it, then go right back to my business at hand.

Suppose you're covering a craft festival, or summer gathering. Not sure what's appropriate? Have you looked at published collections dealing with your theme? You don't have to copy them -- just allow your feelings about that work (what they did right/wrong) help shape your own coverage. Do you have strong feelings about one particular aspect of culture? Some folks might concentrate on the homeless, or bikers, or old men, or children, or, in my case, Punks.... Think about it. Planning will help improve your photography -- and help you concentrate time and resources toward getting the images you really want and need, instead of spraying the countryside for pictures you'll not likely ever look at again, let alone be able to sell to anyone.

Suppose swimming, running, or bike-riding, is your thing. There are good magazines covering all of these. Look at the best published work. Make sure you have mastered the *technical* side of getting those images. Then, with patience (nobody's a "born photographer;" we all start off being pretty *bad*) in time you'll master the field. I learned what pictures horse people wanted by failing to deliver them, and then trying again. It wasn't the equipment, the amount of film, or anything but study and repetition, like learning a new language, or a new musical instrument, and then using it to communicate fluently. Most people don't have the patience to master a new instrument (ever heard a beginner squeaking away on his violin, or her clarinet?) or they're afraid of looking like duffers -- so they don't bother. They use disposable cameras, and produce disposable pictures.

Professionals plan pictures. They may not be as ^&*(*!! pedantic as academics, and their planning may be "in the head," but plan they do. It shows.

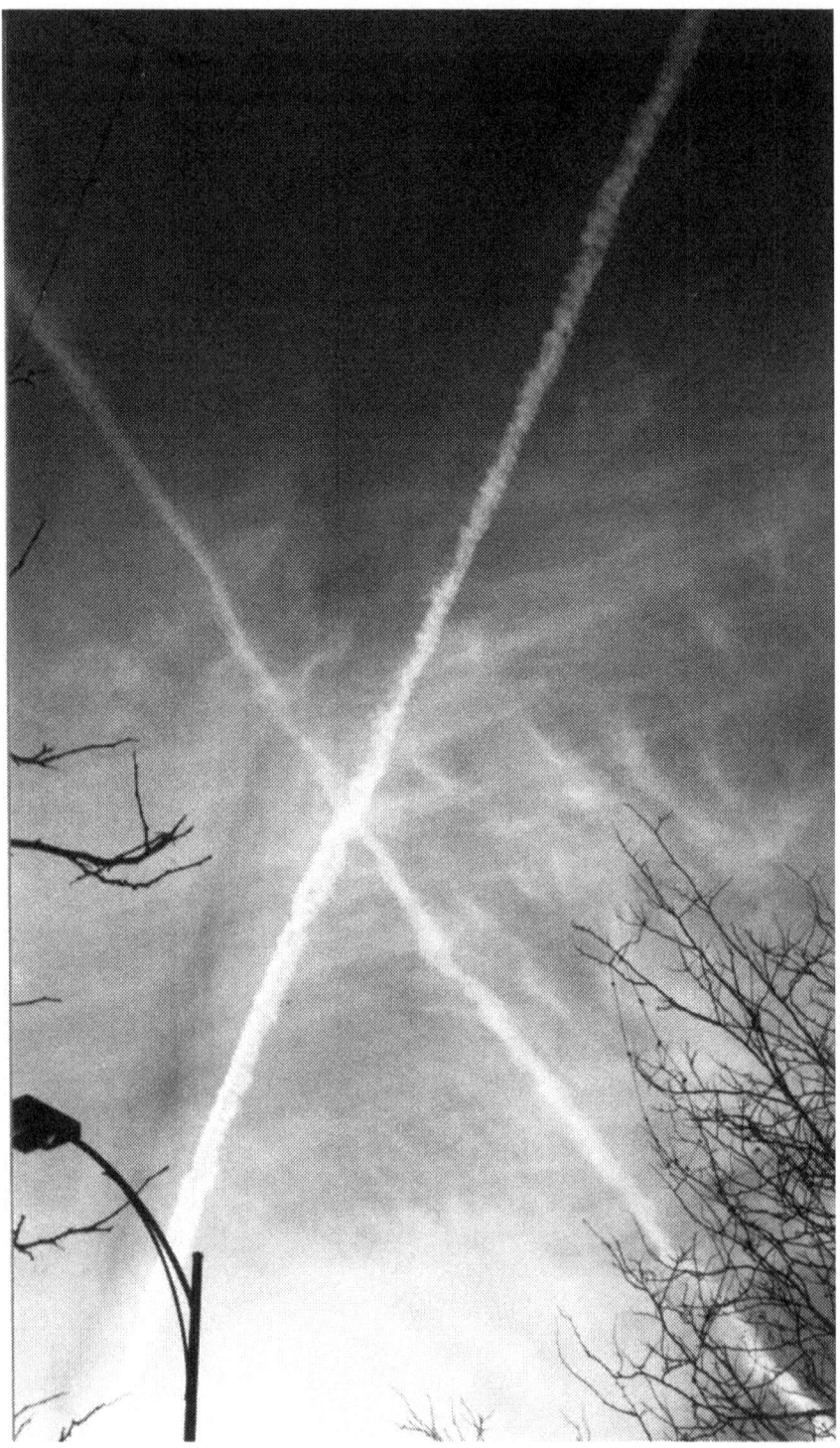

LEARNING COMPOSITION

What is "composition?" Is there a right way and a wrong way? Are there "rules?" Is there a magic answer, something known to Da Vinci, Vitruvius, and Imhotep of Sakkara? *What is this nonsense, and how do I learn "composition?"*

Remember what I said about how a master teacher can only teach you HIS way -- not THE way? Teachers of photographic composition often behave like competing evangelists -- each one claiming "exclusivity," and they would have you believe that the "rules," the "universals" *they* impart to the initiated, are the only legitimate way to play.

Sounds like common, garden-variety bigots, to me...

Do you have to learn a lot of rote rules, to proceed? Are there ten commandments, or fourteen? If you "follow the rules," are you being "creative?" And is anyone who "breaks" them *less valid, less an artist?* No. Look at any comprehensive collection of "masters of photography." Their work is all so different, no one set of composition rules can possibly apply. It's like jazz, again.

"So how do I learn some?" you scream, exasperated with me now. "All this time to tell me *what it isn't*. Tell me what it IS!"

I would teach you composition this way: I would hand you a "reading list" of great photo collections (see Appendix). I would tell you to look at them all, and to single out the photographers whose work moves you. I would ask you to show me the specific images that really grab hold of you -- knowing your closest friend would almost certainly choose a different set of photos.

You start learning by getting clear on what *you like* -- for what good is a set of rules based on someone else's judgement? *Unless **your** heart is in the creative process, unless **you are moved** by what you see, it will all be sterile -- an attempt to please somebody else.* That's not art, and it's not good photography.

So now you can point to 50, or 100 shots, by different masters, that really move you. Next, we "deconstruct" those images -- we take a good look at what is happening in each, and how the photographer got the image. Knowing it's NEVER just "right place, right time," what choices did the photographer make to create the image? What makes *that one* special?

We'll look at the technical side. Was the picture planned, product of much patience? Was it a lucky moment, happening in front of a photographer fully prepared -- to photograph something else?

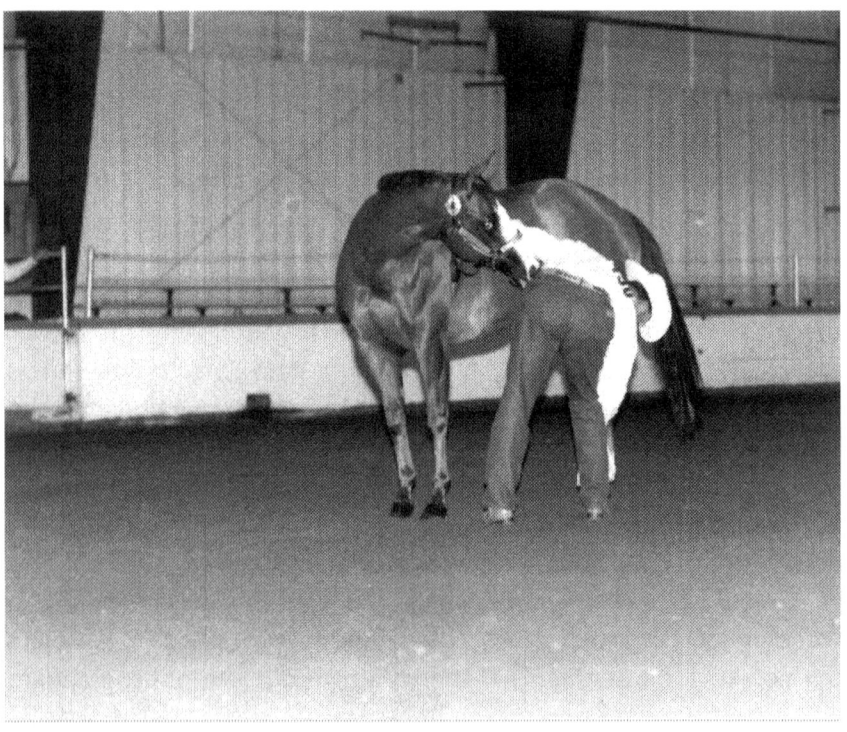

Was choice of film, equipment, exposure, a critical factor? If you can say how the pictures that move you were made, you're getting free lessons from the masters who made them. Isn't that better than some sterile listing of "thou shalt not's" originally compiled for the portrait-painting academies of Second Empire France?

What about me? I was taught composition that way, by saturation in the works of past masters, and, because the man who taught me had been a WW II military photographer, those masters were the ones who'd been *his* examples. I learned from the great ones of the 1930s: Salomon, Capa, Eisenstadt, Bourke-White, Weegee, and the FSA Team (again, see Appendix.) I was training to do *news*, and that means actual content, "news value," transcends composition, but I still learned how a perfect moment takes A picture and makes it THE picture.

But of course I like many different kinds of photos -- and not all of them are "newsworthy." Some of my work is "documentary," in that it, the images, communicate information about the text. My Punk portraits from *Hard Core, Marginalized by Choice* and *Faces of Punk* were meant to show both what Punks do, and that these people are very unintimidating, very much as human as you are. My ongoing documentary at the fishing village of South Gare, in NE England, is meant to highlight details of that picturesque and vanishing lifestyle. Some of my "art" pieces, like "Mad Cow," or the man dancing the Hassipikos with the wrecking ball, are attempts to *seize an amusing moment*, to wring forth a giggle from your stiff, tight lips.

I have other "art" pieces, where the dominant element is *texture* -- either as color change, regularized movement, or the supersharp rendering of actual physical detail, be it water on a flower, broken light through a treetop, peeling paint on an old building, the bark of a tree, or the sweat-drenched skin of a horse. I like texture -- and I do these shots to please *me*. As most of my work is done *to please someone else* (that's how you eat, yes?) perhaps my "texture" work is most clearly my own.

My way of composition can't be your way -- you'll find things that move you that are different, that *don't move me* -- and some of *my* images will leave you cold. *Are you wrong, then? Am I?* No. Like

I heard one singer say: "By all means sing along! If we hit the same notes, that's harmony! If we don't, that's jazz!"

Follow the steps I've laid out. Study. Its a lot of fun to look at great pictures, especially when they're of subjects and events you enjoy. Who were the great photographers of racing? Of sailing? Of small-object technical/archaeological photography? Of dancing? Of different facets of wildlife? There are so many niches -- and the past masters have something to show you, even if you would have approached the same subject matter differently. Its like learning a Coltrane horn solo -- its not yours, but it'll broaden you to have mastered it. Then you can go on developing your own way.

One last thing: Composition is not a "competence," like driving, swimming, riding a horse, or flying a plane. It is an ongoing process. Your way *will* change -- and *you will get better.* There is no "threshold" to reach, but rather a steady consciousness of improvement. Now get with it!

PEOPLE PICTURES

People are funny. Some of them love having their picture taken -- but others blow up. Some will ask you to take their pictures -- or will insist; and others will demand payment, or will threaten to hurt you if you try. It's hard to predict what an individual will do.

What they think of you matters too. If you come on like Joe Nikon, dressed in "Pho-Togs" designer gear, dripping the latest cameras, many folks will freeze up, and either make it impossible for you to get your images, or else they'll start "performing" for you, giving you what they think you want from them, or perhaps what they think you'll pay cash for. But, if they think you're harmless, or as eccentric as they are, or in some other way less than a loud, brash, self-important ego-tripping star reporter wannabee, you can probably get your shots. *Most people find reporters irritating...*

I do Punks. I like them. They know it. That helps (as does the fact that *I've been published before*, and the smell of immortality is intoxicatingly sweet. *PLEEEZE take MY picture!?!*) I also use quite a collection of cameras unfamiliar to youthful eyes, machines by Contax, Exakta, Edixa, Pentacon, Kiev, Kodak, Canon, and Leica. My antiques work, quite well indeed, and often my colorful, ornamented subjects are too fascinated by the appearance and age of my equipment to be much bothered by the fact it is pointed at them. Perhaps they don't find anything that old intimidating? *Never fear a camera older than your father????*

I had to do a series in a Black district of Portsmouth, Virginia. My hirers were out-of-touch yuppies, who hadn't a clue how to reach the people in the neighborhood, and probably would have had apoplexy if they'd met any.

I knew I'd be unable to do my job unless I put some distance between me and them. We parted company. I used some of my older cameras, a pair of Exaktas that looked like dinosaurs had used them for footballs, and left the Nikons at home. I didn't shave, and I wore an old mechanic's shirt with my name on it, a relic from my days as a VW mechanic. I parked my car 2 miles away and walked in. Most of all, I talked to folks, and *I listened.*

It's amazing what folks will tell you and show you, when they think you're on their side. Most of this is anthropology, not photography, but there are two incidents you should hear. In one case, locals took me to see two men, who were selling clothes out of suitcases on the sidewalk. "They're selling stolen goods," I was told. "Take their pictures."

"Why do you want me to....?" I asked.

"Because they're not from here," was the answer.

Another time, my informants asked me if I cared to photograph the "biggest criminal in the neighborhood." They took me to one of those "rent to own" joints that are the bane of a poor man's existence -- and, as I was setting up a shot, the store's gigantic "collector" lurched to the front door and glared at me, nudging my shot into the visual stratosphere. You never know...

We live in suspicious times. It is very hard to hang out in any neighborhood and just photograph, unless the locals know you. You could be a cop, a drug dealer, or a dangerous nut. *I've been mistaken for all of the above...*

There's another thing -- speed. Cameras are irritating. It isn't just the nauseatingly saccharine *"Now say CHEEEEESE!"* we had inflicted on us by clueless parents. **Its having to sit and wait for the jerk to finish fiddling with his @&^%$#** machine! HURRY UP!**

The quicker you can set up the shot, and then PUT IT AWAY, the happier your neighbors will be with you. The better job you do of planning, before you bring the camera out, and the less fiddling about you have to do with it in front of them, the happier your subjects wil be with you, and you may find that critical to your immediate short-term health and safety.

But there's a lot more. What is your attitude toward your subject? If you act like the cat stealing up on the mouse, *like you're a thief, stealing something from your subject, your subject may not be happy with you.* Its not a game -- photography is a *conversation.* Many *papparazzi* get their jaws broken and noses flattened not just because they are there, but because of the predatory bad attitude they show their targets. *They earn those beatings....*

They represent an extreme. To the *papparrazzi,* their targets are "suckers," idiots to fleece, to make a living pirating off of... What do they resemble but the "con-man," looking for folks to rob? *Felonious photography... Is it any wonder some tribal peoples believe to photograph someone is to capture his soul?*

You cannot do good "people photography" without cultivating al least a bit of empathy. Otherwise, the people are just props....

There's a whole lot I could show you, and, out of context, much of it seems trivial -- but it isn't. For instance, your light meter is a racist! Light meters are balanced to for skin tones of 18% gray -- like most Caucasian skin. One day I was assigned to photograph the retirement of a senior police sergeant -- and my editor did not tell me the man was Black. This man was VERY black, the darkest man I'd ever seen, and my light meter just did not provide a realistic reading. What I did was "bracket," take one on, one a stop up, and one a stop under the meter's stated reading. It worked, but a "program" camera's computerized automatic exposure would not have, and such a camera's TTL flash would still have been balanced for white skin. Be aware of this, and do not trust automatic cameras, or hand-held light meters, to be accurate with dark-skinned people.

What lenses are best for people-photography? Most good people work is done at fairly close range, and at ranges nearer than about 6 feet, wide-angle lenses tend to distort. Your subject may seem to have a VERY big nose! Don't do portraits with the wide, unless you mean to be annoying. The 50mm "normal" got its name from being very good for portraiture, and it still is. Most of my

Punk portraits are done with the 50mm. Plus, such a lens is sharp, sensitive (good in low light) and pretty unobtrusive -- just what you need to do people work.

I've done a few with longer lenses, specifically the 90mm and 105mm lengths. Though the 105 is called a "portrait" lens, it is really too long. It doesn't close-focus enough to allow you to really get up on your subject, and to get a good "frame," you have to back way up -- which can break the "connection" between you and the subject. The 105's are sharp, but I seldom carry them on the street.

The 90mm is another story, however, especially the compact 90mm f4s for the Leica and Contax rangefinder 35mms. The 90mm lets me hang back a bit, out of a person's close "personal space," and still do good work. I'm not *sneaking*; rather letting them stay relaxed while I work. A Leica or Contax with a little 90mm is far smaller than a "modern 35mm" with the normal 50mm, is far less obtrusive, and looks so "antique," so "out of time," that Hippies and Punkers are fascinated, especially when I can use my canned spiel about "hand-built, no robots, and nothing plastic." Remember, portrait photography is indeed a conversation, not an act of theft, and anything that improves that conversation is legitimate...

A few years ago, I went to an "Earth Day" festival. These events produce a tremendous number of weekend hippies and dressed-up wannabees -- and make for great photography. There was a "drumming circle," a bunch of guys sitting around beating on drums and feeling profoundly manly. Right. I had the Contaxes, and a Zeiss Super Ikonta folding rangefinder 6x6cm (an ancestor to the Hasselblad). I should point out the event took place literally on the grounds of one of the country's most prestigious Schools of Journalism, and the student photogs were a mite thick on the ground -- all trying to impress each other with their equipment and fashionable presentations. A few of them were staring at me -- wondering what the hell I was carrying?

In the middle of the drumming circle, suddenly appeared a toddler. He stared and stared at the pounding, chanting grown-ups. Then he spotted an unattended drum. Over he went, then sat down and attacked it fiercely. His expression was incredible

-- and I got it. The J-school boys were too busy looking at *me*, to see what I got. My cameras were 50 years older than theirs, and *they* brought home the bacon....

Truism: An old camera that's ready, set, and pointed in the right direction beats the daylights out of the latest model -- that *isn't*. "It's how you play it," my guitar teacher said, so many years ago...

Dangerous locations. If you're in fear for your life, what are you there taking pictures for? Don't you think your fear will color your picture choices? Mightn't it cast your subjects, folks from that "frightening" area, in a bad light? Is that your purpose? Most fear is a little less extreme, more like *heterophobia* (fear of folks not like ME) or fear of robbery/mugging.

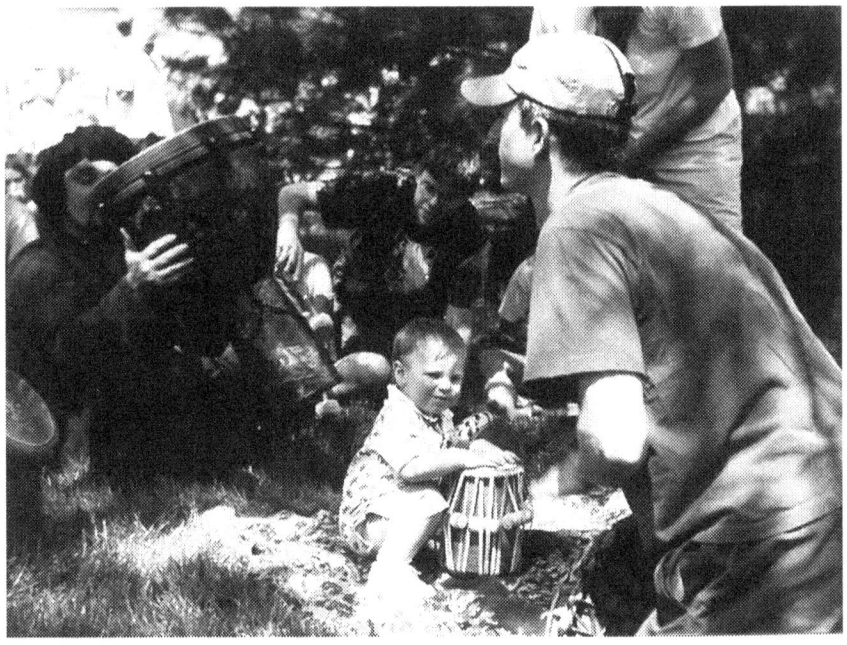

Two things I suggest you do about it: First, if you're that frightened, **don't go there**. Second, **carry less equipment** (*That big bag is NOT for using -- you've got all that stuff with you to IMPRESS, be honest now!*) and be quicker in the use of it. In very tense situations, carry a pocketable camera. I use an old folding Kodak Retina II -- an excellent camera that collapses to the size of a wallet -- and still preserves full function and F2 low-light capability on a 50mm lens.

Are you afraid of your subjects? Why? Have you tried explaining what you want to them -- engaging them in the conversation? A few will say no, but many will help you out. They may well even tell you things you'd never considered. Try it! *Then you can expand this list.*

THINKING ABOUT PORTRAITURE

What is a "portrait?" Is it just a picture of someone? How does it differ from a "snapshot?"

All pictures of people are not portraits. A snapshot of someone in action, even close-up, may even be *called* a portrait, but that is abuse of the term. A portrait is a deliberate and successful attempt to communicate a recognizable likeness, while making a perceived-to-be-true symbolic statement about the viewer.

Compare this to *caricature* and *parody*, where one or more perceived attribute are deliberately overemphasized, so as to provoke amusement and ridicule. Also compare to spot news, sports action, and the snapshot, where an individual is "caught in the act," and the image is always *person + time and place*. These images are, by definition, "dated."

"Formal" photographic portraiture draws on centuries-old traditions of portrait painting. Even the placement of the light is as it was three or four centuries ago. These idealized "heroic" portraits (see the work of Yusuf Karsh) trace lineage back to the statues of classical Greece, which presented an individual (pardon the bad pun) in "the best possible light." Formal portraiture is a very old art form, with very rigid conventions. We call these images "timeless."

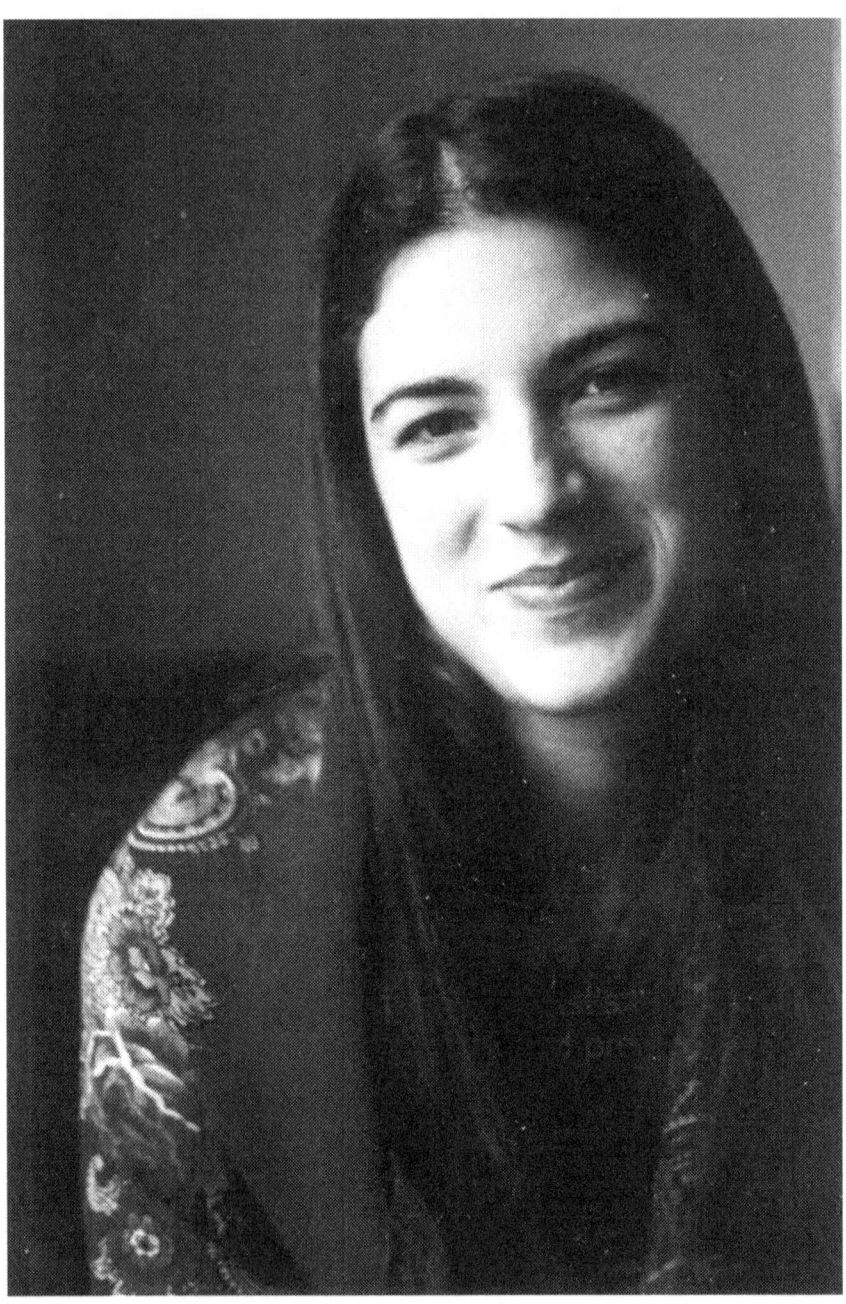

What does "formal" portraiture tell us about the subject? Not much. It is idealized, conventionalized, stylized ... and it seeks to show us someone "heroic," someone "larger than life." We are aware of the different features, perhaps of a wildness in the eyes, but the almost monotonous depiction of subject as *Ubermensch* wears on us. Yusuf Karsh does not tell us much about the individuals he photographs. It is necessary to step downward, toward what I'll call *semiformal portraiture*, to find depiction of real individuality.

Semiformal portraits do not require diplomatic attire, 8" x 10" view cameras, or massive batteries of photofloods, with armies of assistants to manipulate them. In a semiformal portrait, we see simple presentation, good control over lighting and background, minimal "props;" but in an ambience that owes more to good choice of moment than to formal portraiture's total control of the photographic environment.

What the semiformal portrait shares with the formal is an uncluttered background. There may be a few items: a favorite window, a book, a pet, a significant tool -- but it is by no means

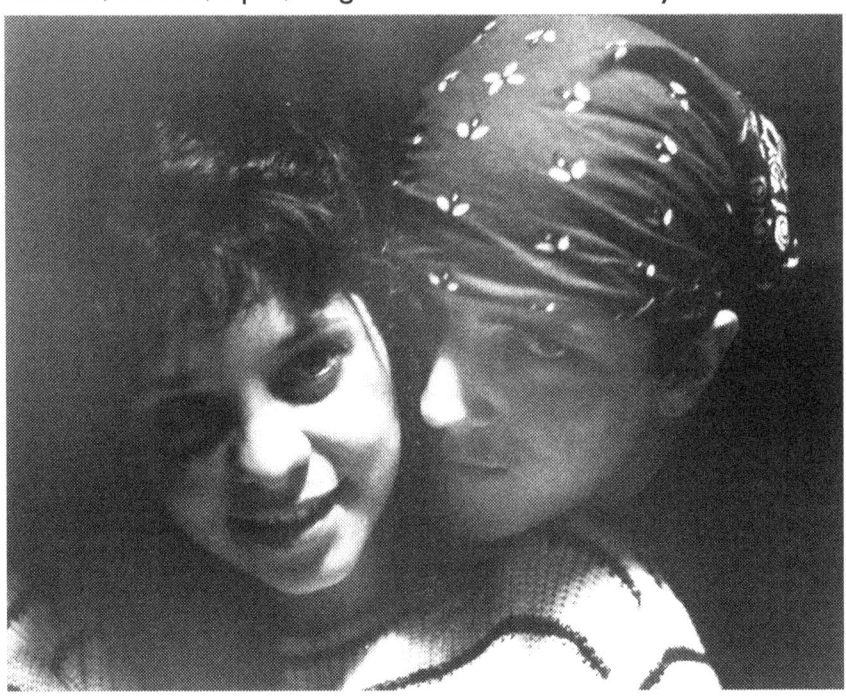

an "action shot." However, there is no attempt to "heroicise" the subject. The semiformal, like the fashion photo, strives to look like a brilliant snapshot. It isn't a snap; it's too much deliberate work for that, but the end product is supposed to convey that impression.

You can do semiformal portraits with simple equipment. Your customers will like them. What do you need to remember?

1. Think about your background. Remember, you can shoot upward, downward, and in any direction -- you should move your subject, and yourself, to maximize the picture. It will matter.

2. Have a concept. Try to previsualize the picture. What do you want it to look like? Planning helps.

3. Avoid wide-angle lenses for portraiture -- they distort a close subject.

4. Be ready. Your subject (unless he/she is a politician running for election right now) would rather not be shuffled about while you make up your mind -- and the process can generate a lot of irritation, which WILL show up in the end product. VERY few photos are helped by irritating the subject.

5. Highlight the good. A semiformal portrait is not an ID "mug" shot, but a piece of technological flattery. *It isn't meant to tell the unvarnished truth.* Find the best way to flatter your subject. It's part of the job.

6. Think about focus. You don't have the big camera and banks of lights available to the formal portraitist, but your pictures will fly or crash on the same criterion as his: sharpness. Make sure the eyes and the mouth are sharp -- as lack of sharpness immediately puts your work into the "Aunt Molly at the beach/box camera" category.

7. Think about exposure. Where the well-equipped snapshooter meters the scene, and lets the camera choose, don't. You have time to get it right; meter the skin tones, not the scene in general. If the subject is darker or lighter than average caucasian, bracket your exposure -- take shots above and below the meter reading as well as on the reading. You want to get those facial skin tones right.

8. Look at other peoples' work. What looks good? Fashion photographers produce excellent semiformals; look at cutting-edge

magazines likw "*W*," and analyse what they're doing.   If you see something you can do better, *do* it.

9.   Practice. Try doing portraits of your friends. They'll love it. And you'll learn.

10. Remember Duncan's Rule: "Get close. Then get closer." The average "portrait" is shot from much too far away. Step in!

And, most of all, **have a sense of humor.** I don't mean *parody* or *insult* your subjects – I mean look for the smile, the laugh, the light, the *life*, the *human-ness*. The world is too full of heroicising, worshipful portraits of jumped-up executives, questionable politicians, and tinpot dictators. Don't add to the mess.

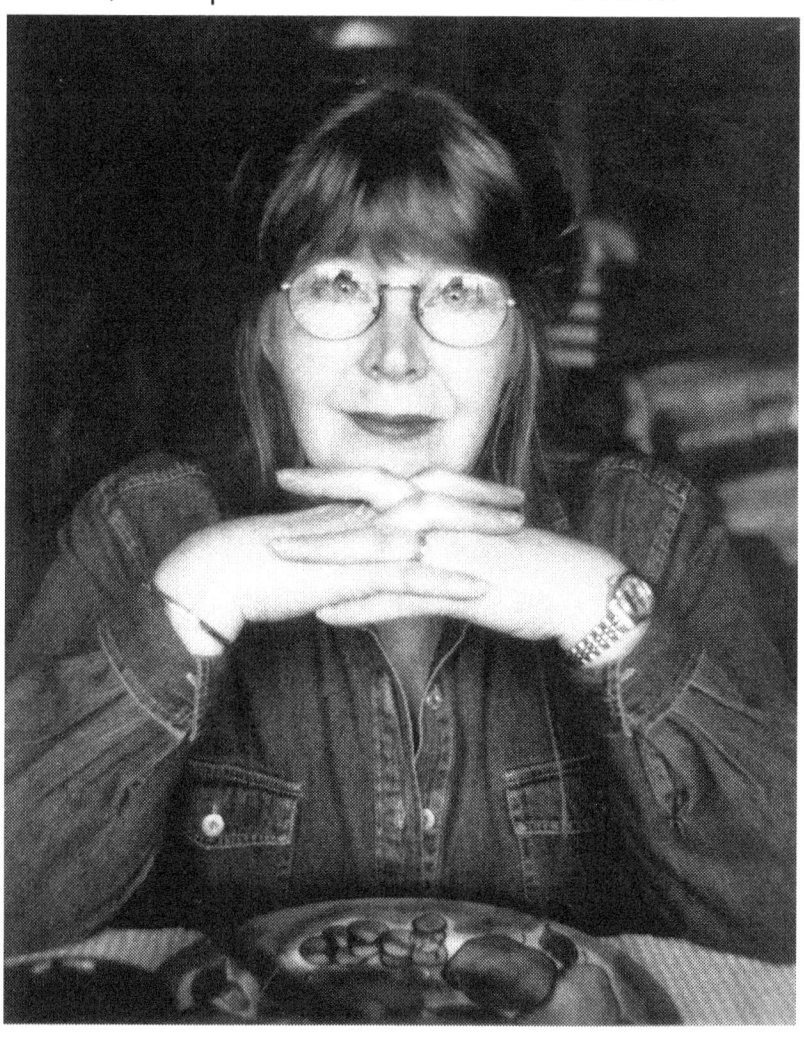

PHOTOGRAPHY AND THE LAW

Photography is not free speech -- not quite. There's a bunch of laws (they differ place to place) and we need to cover a few of the basic principles, for your safety. We'll divide them into *what pictures you can take*, and *what you can do with the pictures*.

First, can you take a picture anywhere you want? No. Without specific permission, you are limited to photographing in public places. If it is occurring in a public place, it's OK. Be careful; what's a "public place?" If you have to pay admission, it is manifestly not "public," and a different set of laws apply.

If you have to break the law to get a picture (IE *trespass*), you're not legally entitled to the picture, any more than a bankrobber is entitled to the fruits of his labor. If you are on private property, and do not have permission to photograph, you have no clear legal right to continue.

What about a ball game? It gets confusing. Some ballparks, like theaters and concert halls, may claim the right to restrict photography -- and it is their right to do so, but, outside that, someone engaging in public performance can be photographed while performing, but not before or after. That ballplayer may be "public" while on the field, but you have no right to follow him home, or to crash his locker-room.

In one case, I saw a heavily-tattooed young man pirouetting on the sidewalk for an admiring young lady. I photographed him, from an upstairs window, with a 200mm telephoto, and the shot wound up in my *Hard Core, Marginalized by Choice*. He was pissed when he found out, but what he'd been displaying in public was fair game for the camera. Had I entered his place of business, and taken such a shot, I'd have been wrong.

An important aside: *You cannot use pictures to defame or libel.* Had I used the young man's image in any way that mocked, lampooned, or insulted him, it would have been his right to sue. Had I used his image on the book's cover, used his likeness to help sell the book, without his express permission, he could have sued. A book's cover art is "commercial purpose," and an individual's likeness cannot be used for commercial purpose (to advertise or sell anything) without that individual's permission.

This leads to the next question: What can you do with the pictures? Obviously, the snapshot you take home and look at will cause you less trouble than the shot you sell to the *Tatler Magazine*, and *that* one will cause you less than the one you decide to use for an advertising campaign, especially if the picture could be perceived as insulting or ridiculing the individual it depicts. Let's go through the stages.

Obviously, **if you commit slander/libel with your camera**, you're gonna get hammered. Don't do it. "Free Speech" laws never have been held to permit slander, and slander with the camera is just as bad as slander with pen or tongue. Stick to how the truth looks, and do not enhance, embellish, or invent.

For selling purposes, a person retains right over his/her own image to a far greater degree than he/she does for news purposes. If I photograph a famous actor drinking a pint of his favorite, I may or may not be in violation, and a magazine like *Us Weekly* may or may not be able to publish it. But, if I use that image to sell brew, or to spearhead an anti-drinking campaign, without the drinker's permission, I'm vulnerable to a lawsuit. Its the "commercial usage" that matters. But note, if it is very smoky there in the pub, and you can't tell just who is there drinking, I may be off the hook -- for if the image "could be anybody," there's no individual protection. Beware, however, of prominently depicting registered trade marks;

those images are protected in much the same way as people's faces.

What's "commercial usage?" Though this may differ place to place, as I understand, commercial usage means *selling*, rather than *documentation*. A picture at a Rock concert is just a picture, but if you put it on an album cover, or a concert poster, it becomes commercial usage. **Models and actors get paid for use of their faces in such** -- whether to sell cigarettes, cars, or cleansing creams.

Taking a picture and hanging it in a photo gallery is not commercial usage -- though making an ad about the show and using the same image in the ad *is*. Using a photo to help present the news is acceptable (as long as it is *honest*), and using a photo to illustrate a scholarly work is acceptable -- though many may differ on just what is "scholarly."

If an image doesn't have a person in it, or a recognizable corporate entity/trade mark, and you did not commit trespass to get it, no problem. If the person in it cannot be recognized, "could be anybody," no problem. If the person is engaging in a public performance, no problem (provided it is in a public location, or the hall allows you to photograph.) If the person allows you to photograph, no problem -- though in some cases you perhaps should get the permission in writing, what we call a "model release." How many of you are likely to follow actors home from the pub, and try to photograph them pissing in the gutter? If you are, I certainly don't want to know you! They call those scum *papparazzi,* "bumblebees," and these creeps feed our appetite for salacious gossip, while hiding behind their organizations' lawyers and fat liability budgets. They damage a lot of lives, and do so because we cluck our tongues in disapproval -- then we hurry to buy the next sheet to see whose space they succeeded in invading *this time*.

Suppose you work with a camera. Who owns your pictures? If you are on a salary, any work you create while on that salary, "in the line of duty," belongs to the organization -- not to you. If you are paid piecework, copyright is yours, unless conveyed to the buyer (read your contracts). If you are an "independent contractor," your pay is not a salary, so the pictures are yours -- unless there is a specific clause in the contract saying otherwise. **Go back and read the contract again.**

Suppose you publish a book, or have an article in a magazine. Read your contract closely! In some cases you will find you have conveyed all copyrights to your publisher. Others will state "one time use," which means the publisher is printing them, but your images cannot be sold on to a third party without your permission (and hopefully without payment of a royalty -- to you.)

These are very muddy waters. My best advice is don't assume anything, read any contracts carefully, ask questions before signing, and do not be afraid to consult an attorney competent in business law.

Good luck!

USING DIGITAL

What is "digital photography?" Should you use it? Will it replace conventional photography? What's wrong with this picture?

Digital photography is the electronic capture and transfer of images. Born of television, it is filmless and more or less instantaneous. Sounds convenient, hey?

It depends on what you want to do. There is this thing called *resolution*. If all you need is coarse, rough images suitable for the web, for e-mailing, or for including in the weekly Advertising Supplement, then you'll find digital photography convenient.

But if you'd use your digital camera, scanner, or computer printer to produce reasonably sharp images, something at least resembling conventional photography, it's another story entirely.

First, how sharp is your computer? Monitors', scanners', and printers' sharpness is measured in "DPI," dots per inch. Conventional cameras' sharpness is measured in "lines per millimeter." It really is the same thing. And there's the problem: If there are 25mm to the inch, a standard resolution of "100 DPI" is how many per millimeter? About 4. An average 35mm camera is capable of about 80 lines per millimeter. The best lenses, 35mm and larger format, are capable of about 120.

But what if you set your digital device for a higher resolution? Try 200 DPI. It looks better, but that's still just 8 lines per millimeter -- well below Kodak's old "snapshot" standard of 40 lines. So raise it further. How about 300 dpi, which is close to the standard resolving limit of many printers? That's 12 lines per millimeter, folks. Twelve. One tenth of what I can give you with a Summicron. **Digital is just not very sharp**.

There's a corollary. To be convenient, to compete with film cameras, a digital camera has to be run in low-resolution (~100 DPI). When you go up in sharpness, the memory-space needed in your computer expands enormously. To manipulate a 300 DPI image, you need *ten times the memory space* your lower-res image takes. Funny, it's not so convenient anymore..... And, a fifty-year old 35mm will far outperform the latest and priciest digital machine.....

But, you may see scanners with "600 DPI" or "1200 DPI" settings. Nice. The file you'd write is so huge you'd need the whole hard drive. Where' ya gonna save it to? How much time do you have, for your computer to process it? Hard drive space? And, many of the "high-res" files are so big the "manipulating" software won't run on them. **If you need real sharpness, digital, as it is today, is <u>not yet practical</u>**. Someday, maybe. And that doesn't even get into the question of digital's limited contrast range (see "zone system.)

One of the reasons digital machines are so cheap is that the manufacturers, knowing they're not very sharp, use cheap plastic lenses on them. You can understand -- the CCD, the electronic substitute for film, isn't very sharp, so why spend money on the lens? *Do you really want one?*

The best digital machines, those with "megapixel numbers" of 8 or better, can set you back thousands of dollars -- and they are still less sharp than a 1937 Leica or Contax -- and will require a big computer, graphical programs, and dedicated printer. Converting to digital? Go get a mortgage, sucker.

So what's it good for? Cataloging, and selling. Those low-res files don't take too much space, and you can keep collections of them on hard drive. They print reasonably, and you can e-mail them. They are just the thing for offering to a buyer, to say: "OK, here it is. Are you interested?"

That's what I use it for. Once a new way of handling the huge memory requirement imposed by truly sharp digital, once digital can match traditional image quality, THEN I shall consider it. It probably will happen someday, but I'm a user, not a techie -- and I need sharp pictures *now*. So do you.

Shipping Digital Images

Whether you are a digital photographer or not, you will periodically find yourself sending and receiving digital images, eiter on line or by media such as the CD-ROM. There are a few things you should remember.

First, there are a number of "image protocols," the most popular being GIF, TIF, and JPG. Which one does your customer want? ASK ASK ASK! If no one has a clue, send JPG -- it has good, broad utility.

Second, what "resolution" does your customer want? Although on-line images average between 72 dpi and 100 dpi (that's all the better a screen can render), such coarse images are completely inappropriate for paper printing -- where the minimum ("newspaper") resolution is 200 dpi or better, according to the printers of the *New York Times*. For a "slick-paper" magazine, you'll need more like 400 dpi -- and some of their editors want you to send them a TIF file. TALK TO THEM!

Some people's software won't open a TIF file....

Remember, once you scan an image into your computer, you cannot change the resolution -- so save with sufficient resolution! Save everything at 400 dpi, and you should be OK.

The opposite extreme is bad too. Some folks will try to send you images at 5000 dpi, for whatever reason, but this just clogs computers and irritates people. It is not necessary (your high-end laser printer probably can't render better than 1200 dpi at "fine" setting; many lasers "max" at 600 dpi) and wastes everybody's time -- so it is bad for repeat business -- they'll use someone else next time!

Another no-no is images-in-text. It is very hard to get an on-screen image sent to you in text, back out to a file, so you can use it. Some folks' e-mail handling programs block these images, treat them as viruses, or reduce them to pages and pages of alphabet noise. It takes space, slows down computers, and makes extra work. If you are shipping an attached file, resist temptation to have it on screen too -- let the customer download it and open it in their own good software.

Ask! Find out! Know!

ABOUT "SHARPNESS"

"Hey, that looks really sharp," we say, looking at a new car, a new suit, or a new tattoo. *Sharp* means "neat, good, special...." We like *sharp-ness*.

What about *photographic* sharpness? What is it? Is it just one thing?

Turns out there are a lot of different factors affecting whether or not a picture "looks sharp." The primaries are:

Camera or subject movement
Lens sharpness
Quality of processing
Quality of film

The fastest way to have an unsharp picture is to wiggle. If the camera is in motion when the shutter opens, everything it records will be more or less a blur, depending on the speed of the shutter. That's why so many professionals use tripods and monopods wherever possible, to steady their cameras. "Camera movement" is a picture-wrecker.

Sometimes you'll see a shot where almost everything is sharp, but just maybe one object is a blur? That's *subject* movement. To deal with it, you can pick a better moment, you can use a faster shutter speed, or you can "pan," move with the subject. Then there is *lens sharpness*, also known as *resolving power*. Cheapo box cameras, film or digital, have lenses that aren't very sharp. Measured in "lines per millimeter" (very similar in concept to the "DPI" measurement used to rate digital cameras and scanners), this means a better lens will have a higher number. How much higher? Cheap boxes might resolve 25 -- and the best cameras might resolve 120.

There is also *contrast*. If there is a visually crisp distinction between the dark and the light, the apparent sharpness will be higher -- the photo will look sharp. Light "bounces" down the barrel of a lens, and straight lines can tend to be refracted a bit, especially in an older, "uncoated" lens. Although the uncoated lens may be, strictly speaking, just as sharp as the coated one, or sharper, than the coated, its higher "flare" content makes it look less "sharp." Since "sharpness" is really a value judgement about what something looks like, rather than a measurable statement of scientific fact, coatings sell.

Different films have greater or lesser contrast. DO NOT automatically assume that more is better -- very high contrast films can look like bad '60s Pop Art. The more "high-contrast," the less subtle detail. Remember your "zone system?" Higher contrast films (especially the fashionable "high saturation" stuff) are not kind to nuances, and in fact are expressly formulated to "rev up" primary colors so as to compensate for poor equipment and bad exposure. Thus you'll see they have far fewer zones than do the lower contrast films. "High-sat" is a shuck job -- but it's now damn near the only game in town. My choice is to use the lower ASA ("slower") films with lower saturation, and go for *real* sharpness.

There's another issue -- bad processing. Cheapo cheapo processing houses have to buy chemicals too -- and, short of using slave labor, the best way they have to save money is to change chemicals less often. This they do. Perhaps it would be better if they used fresh solutions after 60 rolls? Every roll past #60 they can get out of that "soup" is gravy. If it looks funky, no matter, they'll tell you it was a *bad exposure* -- and you'll believe them! And sometimes it *is* a bad exposure -- *theirs*, too much or too little time in the enlarger.

One last factor -- grain. Film, like a computer screen, is made up of dots. The techies call them "pixels." The bigger the pixels, the fewer of them per inch, and the less sharp it looks. "Fast" film, with higher sensitivity to low light, has bigger grain. Use it, and it looks "grainy." Generally the slower a film's "speed,", the less grainy its appearance.

See what I mean, sharpness is complicated? There is no substitute for learning.

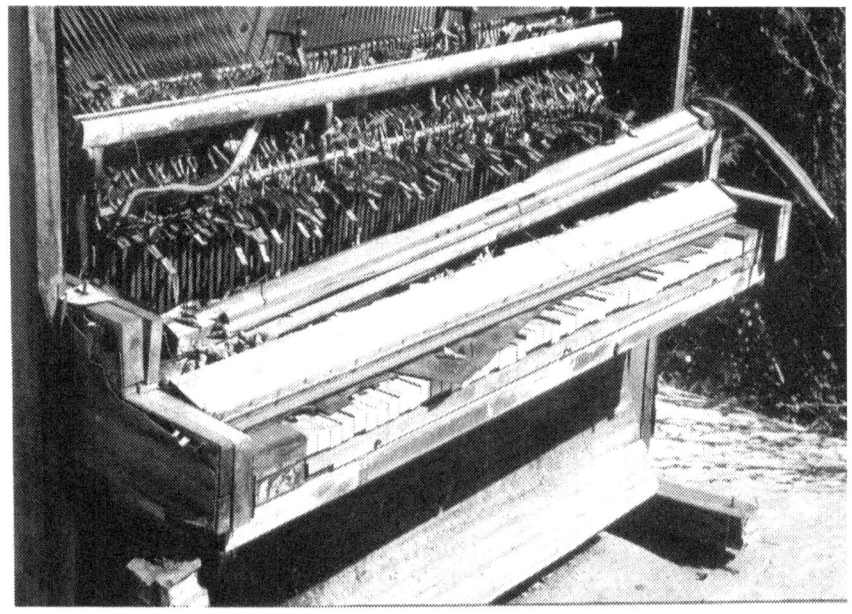

SEEING AND MEANING

What does a picture *mean*? Does it mean the same thing to different viewers? Can you predict what a picture will mean, when the viewer is someone you've never met?

Elsewhere, we've discussed the "snapshot." It is a picture *of something*, and it has no meaning outside of identity: "Here's aunt Martha..." or "This is Carrie on her honeymoon in 1959." *Identity.*

Part of composition is the *establishment of meaning*. The picture you've envisioned/created *means* something, stands for something, *evokes something*. Hopefully. Start with yourself, the creator. If it doesn't move *you*, why should it move anybody else? The world is full of visual mung -- don't add to the collection!

OK. So now you're square on what you're trying to say with a picture. Hopefully you're not trying to say too much with your picture. The best photos, the ones that win awards, do not send complex messages, but simple and clear ones. Yours should too.

Now. Why should someone else, looking at your picture, get the same meaning you did? Pictures don't come with signs attached. There is no caption telling the viewer what it means!

How do we get meaning from a photograph? When we're beyond *identity* ("here's a shot of Adolf Hitler" is identity), pictures communicate meaning *via analogy*, as *symbols*. We see a specific person, place, or object, which by analogy evokes a response, and that response is much more broad-based. The picture of lovers kissing may make us think of our own experiences; the bombed-out church may inspire reflections on the cost and folly of war; the old house may evoke our own childhood memories.... But....

Do all viewers have the same response to the same picture? Of course not. Certain pictures are "universal" enough that many different viewers are moved by them, in more or less the same direction. These pictures wind up endlessly replicated, of course -- at the expense of other, more original work. Dorothea Lange, who produced many such, disgustedly called them "cookie cutters."

But meaning is observer-applied, and most of the time a different observer will derive different meaning. A flag is a good example: What do you think when you see the American flag? Would you be surprised to find that a Ukranian, a Frenchman, or a Senegalese, looking at the Stars and Stripes, reacted differently? Of course not! Same with pictures.

I'll give you a few images that evoke different meanings to different viewers. First, the Cheyenne horseman in his finery, with his long lance. Tied to the lance... are scalps. What meaning do you derive? Now, what if you were there, and you were another Cheyenne? What if you were a missionary, and one of those scalps was your daughter's?

Or the jungle of New Guinea, and there, in a clearing, is a longhouse. On the step sits an old man, smoking his pipe. Above him, in a basket, are skulls, swinging gently in the breeze... What if you were there, an emissary from another tribe? Or from his own? Or knew one of your ancestors lost his head to this man? *How the meaning changes...*

Pictures can be ambiguous. I don't point this out to say "give up trying to convey meaning," but rather that the photograph, however powerful, is an imperfect and imprecise tool for conveying meaning to the stranger. The better you know an audience, and the more they are like you, the easier it is to communicate with them. That's obvious, hey? Imagine you're a "deadhead," a follower of the Grateful Dead, and you took a few shots that really encapsulated what a joyous occasion that concert was. Another deadhead would probably "get it," derive the same meaning looking at your pictures that you did. But, show them to the cop on the beat, or Sergeant-Major Jones, USMC. What meaning do you think *they'll* get?

How the meaning changes...

What do you do about it? Be aware, know what you're trying to communicate, keep it simple, simple, simple, and don't be surprised when strangers derive a different meaning than the one you intended. At least they were moved sufficiently to derive a meaning at all!

Semiotics, the anthropological study of signs, symbols, and meanings, is a huge, fascinating field. Unfortunately, most of the writing on semiotics is pretty opaque, to put it nicely, but you have the basics, right here.

THINKING ABOUT
THE ZONE SYSTEM

Ansel Adams made beautiful pictures, didn't he? So did his competitors: Edward Weston, Minor White, Paul Caponigro..... but, more than these guys' skill at composition (which was tremendous), the textbooks are all honking on about something they call the "Zone System." Can you describe it? I can't, not really.

It's about exposure and contrast. We know that much. What do you know about a film's **range**? Range is the distance a film can accurately cover between the brightest item in a picture and the darkest (and I mean light intensity, not color). If a person is standing under a bright light on a dark street, if you expose and print for the street, the figure will look like Hollywood angel, all burned out. If you expose and print for the figure, the street will be black, without detail. The contrast in the picture **exceeded the film's range**.

Most range problems are not so extreme, but you still need to think about them. First, what about your light meter? What does it measure? Some cameras have **averaging** light meters. *Konica*, old *Leicaflex*... The meter looks at the picture area, or most of it, and reads the total falling on that area. Most hand-held meters, like my *Lunalux*, do the same. Nikon cameras, all but the newest, use a "**center-weighted**" metering, where the middle of the picture is treated as "more important" by the meter. A bright face in a dark window will be correctly exposed.

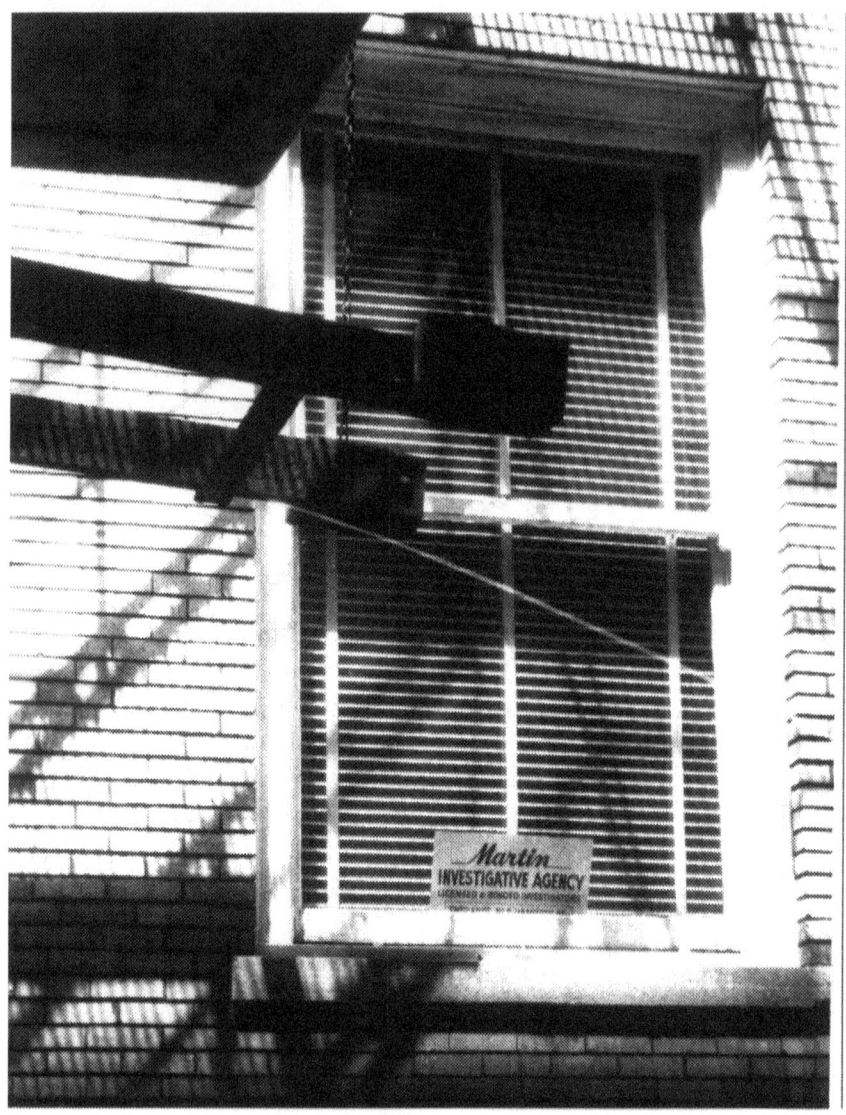

Then there is the **spot meter**, reading only a small percentage of the center of the picture, and nothing else. Also there is the "matrix" meter, where the picture area is divided into 5 or more areas, and, depending on your camera's "program," a balance is struck between the lightest and the darkest, according to what somebody at the factory programmed into your camera's computer.

It does just fine for snapshots of Aunt Molly.

Did Weston use a meter? Did Eugene Atget? Brassai? Did Adams? Walker Evans? Minor White? These guys looked at their subject, looked at the brightest and the darkest, and, as they'd spent years in the darkroom, they knew exactly what would work on the negative and what they could print. Now "zones," as they used the word, were the visible "steps" between the lightest and the darkest objects/areas in the print. One of their goals was to get as many zones as possible in a print.

That takes a lot of work, and it's much easier with a big camera, the kind you probably don't have. But there are some things you can take into account.

First, remember "fast" film? The stuff they charge a buck more for a roll of? "Stop-action" and all that? Well, it has less range than the slower stuff. The slower, cheaper film **does a better job** with the distance between maximum and minimum brightness, B&W or color. And, different films of the same nominal "ASA Speed" will have different ranges -- this is one time the advertisers are right -- it DOES make a difference.

Now we approach a good old-fashioned All American shuck-and-jive job: "High Saturation." It is my contention that Americans are such knee-jerk "consumers" that all you have to do is start yelling "bigger, better, higher," and you got it sold. Why should "higher" not be better than "lower?" Sell sell sell! *Not in my consumerist world...*

Well, it isn't. High-saturation is a way of revving up the primary colors, the bright reds, oranges, yellows, etc, by losing the subtleties between them. Lose the fine shades; build up the primary colors.... An English girl with pale freckles is rendered white-faced. A sunset is simply a blaze of orange. May I be assured if you were satisfied by such, you'd not be reading this? *"Digital" people, your gear has no range to speak of.*

High-sat is pure mickeymouse, but it has the marketing muscle of Mama Kodak behind it, and Mama is perfectly capable of designing something more convenient *for them*, then telling *you*, with a billion-dollar ad campaign, that it's something you can't live without. Hey. You can. Count on it.

True to form, if you want old fashioned "natural" (low-sat!) colors, Kodak will sell you a high-priced "professional" film that will give you what you always had -- for four times the price! Or you can go look at the films made by those behind-the-times eastern Europeans. They're cheap. And, your pictures won't look like an advert for candyland. They have more range. They produce more zones....

In cheapo-cheapo doublespeak, there's another word for range. They call it "exposure latitude." That means how far you can screw it up and still get a usable picture. Great. Sell me film based on how much an idiot you think I am? Or is it how much of an idiot you want to convince me that I am? For buying your insinuation that I'm too effing dumb to do it right the first time? It's not soap, Jack.

If you take a film with a lot of range, a lot of exposure latitude, and expose/process it correctly, you will get the maximum zones, the broadest possible spread between the brightest and the darkest. You should also get the broadest and most life-like range of colors. ANY film will work at its best when correctly exposed, but all films are not created equal: The low-ASA, "slow" emulsions produce more range, less grain, and more color than the "faster" films.

Why did the old masters' prints look so good? These were brilliant, highly skilled artists, working slowly and carefully, with large cameras. They did it all themselves. They did not depend on light meters, programmable cameras, or discount processing houses.

It's no surprise their pictures look great.

THINGS THAT MOVE

Since photography began, successful pictures of *motion* have been one of its biggest challenges. We all know about *camera motion* -- what happens to the picture when you, the photographer, can't hold still. But what about *subject motion?*

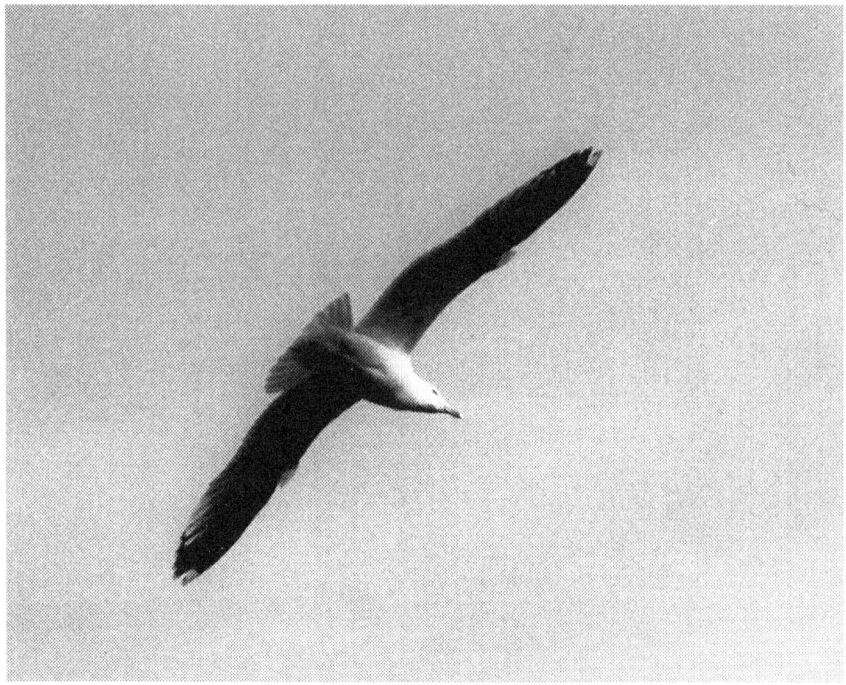

The earliest photographic plates were so "slow," took so long to "gather an image," that absolute "hold it right there!" stillness was necessary. Portrait photographers had iron neck-braces, like torture devices, to make sure their subjects sat still. Battle pictures prominently featured corpses -- *they* don't move. Horses were photographed standing, not at the gallop.

"Faster" films and better lenses allowed photography of motion. People took cameras up in balloons, and invented aerial photography. Oskar Barnack took the first 35mm aerial photos, from a zeppelin. Young Jacques Henri Lartigue took his 4x5 cameras to the auto races. And a great many photographers went out into the middle of World War I.

These were the first folks to deal with the problems of *photographing motion*. What they learned -- still matters.

You know that a speeding object, correctly exposed, but with a slow shutter speed, will be a correctly-exposed *blur*. With a faster shutter speed, you can "freeze" action. Of course there are matters of degree, and you have to decide how fast, how much "freezing' you want.

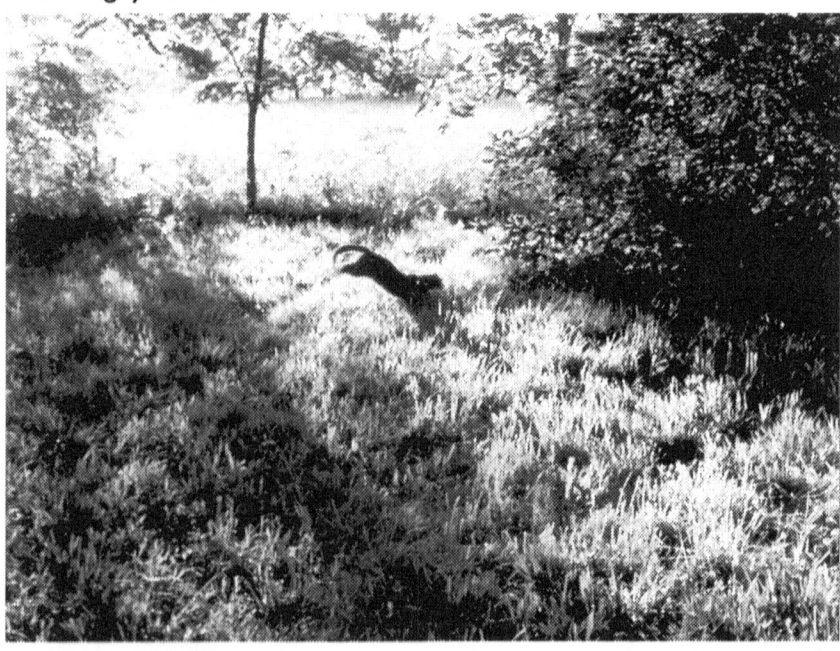

Judgement calls like this help keep photography interesting!

Then there is "panning." Instead of waiting for the subject to come to you, waiting for the moment (and catching a perfectly-exposed blur as it hurtles past a sharp background), you pick up your subject well short of the target, and stay on it, swinging with it, like a B17 machinegunner. What you'll get is a sharp subject against a blurred background. It'll sell.

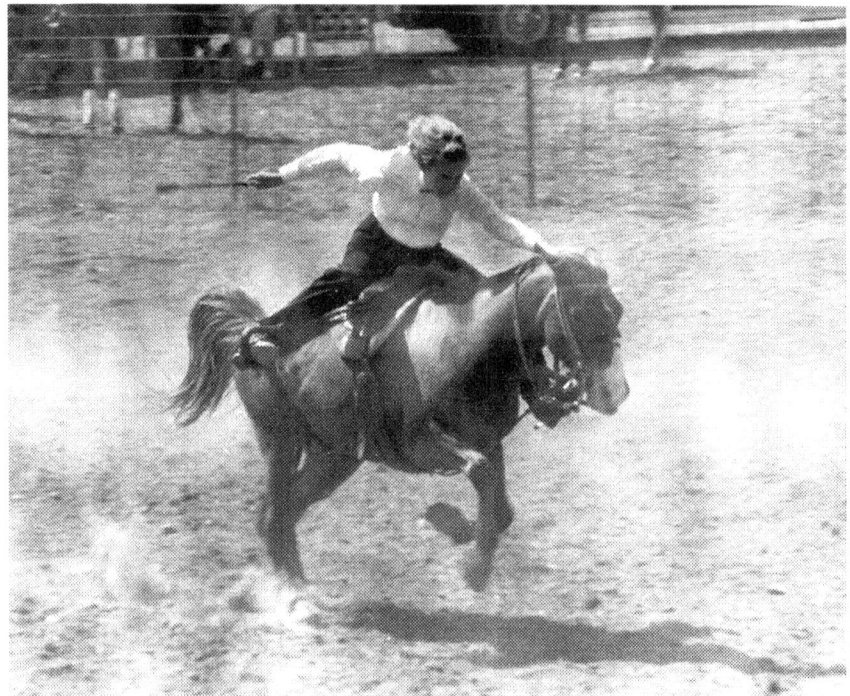

You can do running people, horses, notorcycles, race cars, even aircraft flying a predictable course, with this method. Try and get on the inside of any curve they're making, if you can.

What about "fast film?" The purpose of faster film is the chance to use a higher shutter speed, cutting the risk of blur. How important is it to stop motion? Will you be hand-holding long lenses? There's nothing more destructive than camera movement -- so if it is a risk, faster film is insurance. But, "fast" film comes with a price, in several ways. First, it costs more. Second, it has less latitude -- meaning you have to do a better job exposing it, and third, it has less richness and range than its slower equivalents. Those who use "fast" film all the time, without cause, are harming their wallets -- and their pictures.

I've done horses. Consider a barrel-race. The horse comes out of the gate, breaks right, circles a barrel, dashes to the left, circles a second barrel, dashes to the center, circles a third, then dashes back to the gate. To shoot this, I used Nikon FEs, auto exposure, motor drive, with 80-200mm zoom lenses. They're one-touch zooms, too; a push zooms them and a turn focuses them. I like these lenses loose, where a purist would say they were "worn out." Nothing wrong with the focus when a zoom is loose, but it becomes very easy to stay with a moving target. Use auto exposure here! Too much is too much -- concentrate on timing; let the camera do the dirty work. Let the motor do the winding (but don't shoot the whole roll in 2 seconds), and you'll be surprised what you can do. It takes practice -- so do so.

There is time and place for camera motion; shots like this one.

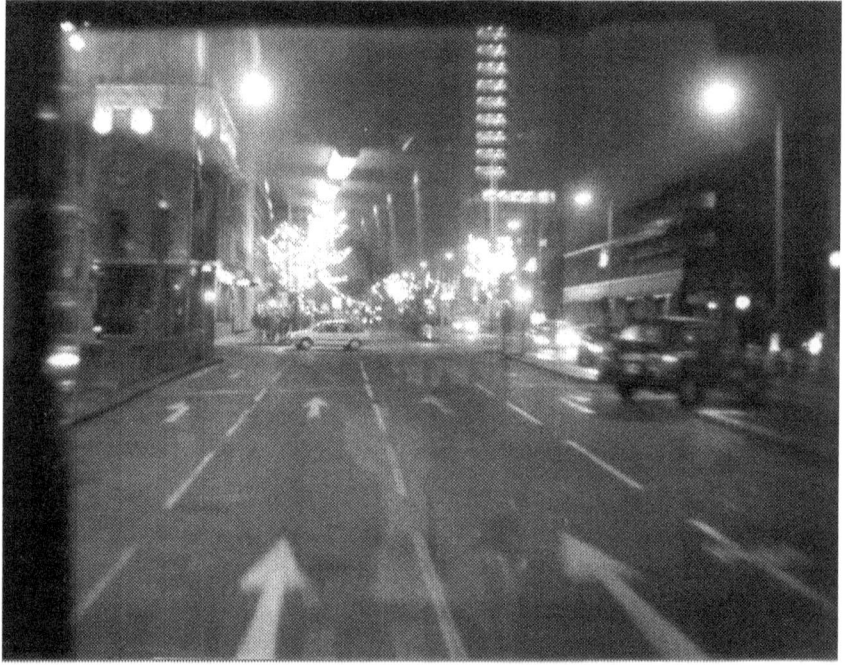

They are limited, specialized, "artsy," and should be the exception, not the rule. *Maybe some band's album cover?*

There is no way to "cook-book" this, or any of photography's other problems. Photography is art, not science, so almost everything you do is a judgement call. I guess that's why its interesting?

WILDLIFE PHOTOGRAPHY

Do you like to hunt? Do you enjoy moving slowly and quietly through the woods, in pursuit of an elusive animal? Could you sit for hours in a camouflaged blind, waiting for that once-in-a-lifetime shot? Above all, are you *patient?*

This might be your niche.

Wildlife photography cannot be hurried. For all but the finest "big name" shooters, the financial rewards are far out of step with the time investment required to produce them. You have to do it for *love.*

I'm serious. Wildlife work is a test of the depth of your motivation.

Are you at home in the outdoors? The skills of the hunter: orienteering, tracking, and survival, are of equal use to the wildlife photographer. No city-dweller can expect brilliant success from his tour-bus window, regardless what the travel agent says. *Learn* about the environment, the weather, and the habits of your prey -- first. Then go. Don't just "visit" -- you have to *live there.*

You need rugged cameras -- Nikons or Leicaflexes. The working conditions are almost as bad as wartime, and anything less than 100 percent reliable means lost pictures. You need cameras that can "take it." *And you'd better be in good physical shape yourself.*

You need sharp, easy, quick-handling long lenses. That means "standard" telephotos, not zooms; they're too slow, too heavy, and too unsharp. It also means "factory," as so many after-market pieces are neither sufficiently robust nor reliable. You wouldn't go hunting with a trash firearm; don't hunt for bloodless trophies (especially as the picture of an animal can earn you far more money than can its corpse) with substandard, bargain-basement equipment. And those 2x and 3x "tel-extenders? WAY too unsharp -- and you won't sell anything they produce.

And please -- learn how to use your stuff before you take it to the woods!

What do I have? I have a pair of fast (f2.8) 180mm short telephotos. I have a quick-handling Novoflex "follow-focus" 300mm (the German inspiration for the Russian "Fotosniper"), a somewhat impractical, but extremely sharp Leitz 280mm with Visoflex adapter (for the old screw-mount cameras), and a 500mm Nikon "mirror" lens. In bright light, I've got it covered. In low light, my fast 180s do an excellent job, but they're really better for the circus than they are for the woods; It's work to get close enough. And I have tripods.

If you can get close enough that you don't need a tripod, you're at the zoo. Long lenses magnify camera shake. No one wants unsharp animal photos -- you need a heavy tripod, a light tripod (for backpacking), a monopod, and a beanbag.

What's a beanbag? A soft bag, perhaps 12" x 6" x 2", half full of dried navy beans, upon which you can rest a camera with telephoto for shake-free exposures. Try it!

You've got to keep that camera still; how else are you going to do it? I know, you think you can hold it steady... but, no, you can't. Maximize your chances of taking a good sharp photo -- and use a tripod, monopod, or beanbag.

Film? The best wildlife shots have deep rich color, which means Fujicolor or Ektachrome/Kodachrome slides. (Some editors *require* slides -- and you'd better know before you go. Ask!) Film speed is less important, unless you are planning on working in consistently bad light. You want a quality film that gives accurate color rendition across all ranges. You want one that has some latitude (meaning you can be off a stop or two and still look good -- and all films with the same ASA do NOT have the same latitude) and you want consistency.

There is no magic film. I'd carry bricks of Kodachrome 200 (a personal favorite) or Fujicolor 200. Another would have his reasons for carrying something else.

For good flash work of wildlife, you need astounding luck, the patience of Job, or a good taxidermist. Don't count on it. Shoot by available light.

What's a "good" wildlife photo? It's one that makes you feel something. Look at the work of Rod Brindamour or Hugo Van Lawick. Their animals are not just clear, sharp, and well composed. Great photography is a masterful presentation of intangibles -- and these men's pictures grab at your soul.

I suggest you do as with learning photo composition -- study the work of the masters, decide which shots move you, then learn how they were made, and follow on that long and dusty path.

The rewards are great.

ROCK AND ROLL

"I do the Rock," sang Tim Curry, with great enthusiasm, some years ago. It's hard not to be enthusiastic about taking a camera to a Rock Concert -- but so often the pictures don't measure up to the fun we had taking them. Sound familiar? If you want to "do the Rock," and have pictures worth showing, there are a few things to remember.

In the beginning, people played gigs outdoors, in the daylight. That's rare now. If you're lucky enough to find such a concert, you just need the appropriate lenses -- recognizing your neighbors may not appreciate a long telephoto, and the promoter may not allow you a tripod or monopod. Plus, they're hard to dance with....

Most concerts take place under lights. (*Duh....*) This is where it gets fun. People think that because the lights go down, and then the band appears, that it's *dark* up there. No, it *isn't*. Those stage lights are very bright. If you've guessed an exposure, based on a dark stage, you'll be wrong.

Should you flash? No, no, and no! First, the musicians hate it -- and you might get thrown out. Second, most flashguns have an effective range of 8 feet (that's why professionals carry huge flashguns that reach out 50 feet -- and *how* far away did you say your seat was?) and third, the light show is half the fun! When you flash, you kill all the pretty colored lights. Unless you have a stage pass, and are so good with fill-flash that you'd not be reading this book anyway, leave your flashgun at home.

What about those lights? Like I said, they're bright. And (long *Duuuuh!*) they *change* a lot! That means fun with light-meters! Recommendation: The warmup act is there to make sure the lights and PA are working. Take some meter readings while the amateurs are up there. Note them, and use them -- then you have a better idea of settings.

Automatic and "program" cameras are optimized for "normal" scenes -- and there's nothing "normal" at a Rock concert! If you let your camera decide what to set, expect it to set wrong. You need to go "metered manual" (match-needle, like an old Nikkormat) or use a hand-held meter.

Do you need "super-speed" film? No. Like I said, it's bright up there. Plus, something they don't tell you, the slower color negative (C41) films have more "exposure latitude," which means you can miss the precise settings and still get a good shot. Forget slides -- with them you have to be very precise. Concerts are too much fun to have to worry about being precise...

What kind of camera? Focusing is a problem in the dark. Ideally, I'd choose a high-end rangefinder camera with a fast short telephoto (the Contax with a 90mm f2 or the Canon 7 with an 85mm f2). Why? Rangefinders resolve one point of light -- so all you need is a single highlight to aim at -- while SLRs require you to resolve the scene -- and with all the lights, motion, noise, and general intoxication, this may not be possible. Plus, my Canon 7s are small and light, and don't look intimidating, and my Contaxes are so wierd-looking (to today's eyes) that no one takes them seriously. Many professionals choose M-Leicas -- and if you have the money, these are a bit better than the Canon 7s (and certainly newer!)

Can you reload your camera in the dark? You better learn how, before you take it to a Rock concert.

Recommendation: Films come in 24 exposure and 36 exposure sizes -- and for concerts, use the 36-exp size. It cuts down reload time. Use that time getting shots you'd have missed.

I remember covering a *Golden Earring* concert (my age is showing...?), and I had been briefed that at the end of the last song, the drummer would jump over his kit -- and a shot was wanted. Thus I was ready. If I hadn't known it was coming, would I have been set up and ready? Probably not. Moral: A little knowledge of the band you're covering is a very good thing! Why do so many folks have pictures of the *Who* bashing their instruments? Because everybody knew it was coming. Be ready.

Another recommendation: Probably because of jerks with flashguns, some venues prohibit cameras at all. I've been to a few, and its a pain to have to get out of line and go park cameras in the car -- worse if you planned on getting paid for the pictures -- plus there are big dudes just aching for someone to throw out, so don't cheat. Ask, when/before you buy tickets! I was at a Santana show where we were all patted down like terrorists (and the same hardboys were patting down both sexes, so it wasn't to cop a feel!) and you'd have a rough time sneaking in your favorite camera -- and, you might just lose it.

If I was going to do a concert, like I said, I'd use my Canon rangefinder cameras. I'd forget flash (unless I was going to be on stage, or interview bandmembers after), and I'd use slow color negative film. I'd think of my film budget, and then triple it (we always estimate about 1/3 of our needs!) I'd carry a fast wideangle (35mm f1.8) and a normal (50mm). I'd use a fast 90mm short tele too, and I'd have at least two camera bodies. I'd leave the motor-drive zoom-lens SLR's at home -- you're there to get pictures, not to impress. I'd pull out a few CDs from the band (or go buy them) and have a good listen. Do you have friends who've been, who've seen them? Ask what happened. Be ready. (Long before I took cameras to a Mosh, I was briefed in detail on what a Mosh was!)

I wouldn't drink, and I wouldn't smoke any dope. Photographers can get busted too (I've seen it -- from 2 feet away!), and there are LOTS of reasons for you to stay sober while you're working!

Does this sound "un-spontaneous?" Tough. My cameras cost a lot more than my Audi, and when I take them out, it's to produce something with them. For me, it's fun -- but it's like hunting -- there's a discipline, and I accept it. Good Rock photos are precious, and what you can get -- others WILL want. Good luck.

AERIAL

Aerial photography is an adventure. There you are, leaning out of a rickety biplane, snapping pictures that reveal the precise location of the missing treasure..... Right.

Aerial photography is a lot of work. It's expensive to get up there, your time is short, and it's awfully easy to screw up and blow it all. *"We don't want excuses; we want pictures!"*

Let's talk about aerial photography. People have done good work with cameras in aircraft (and *balloons* -- Oskar Barnack took the first 35mm aerial shots, from a zeppelin, in 1915), and, in good light, some of the big old "press cameras" (4x5 inch and larger) can outperform the best of today's 35mm mini-marvels.

But there's a lot to think about. Let's start with the obvious -- suppose you want an aerial shot of some particular place or action. First, can you (and your pilot) *find it from the air?* Does your pilot know where it is? Will you recognize it, when looking down at it from above? *This can be embarrassing -- when you pay $100 per hour, and can't find the target!*

Will the light be good? Bad weather, clouds, fog, too early, too late... It all gets in the way of getting a good picture.

Will you have enough time over the target? One pass won't cut it. You'll need to fly over it several times, 'til you're sure you got it.

What kind of film? Do you need "fast film?" Remember aerial work is about *detail*. You need all the detail-handling capacity a film can give you -- and the slower the film, the more detail it can render.

OK, shutter speed. Airplanes jiggle, vibrate, and buzz. Small ones jiggle worse, and the closer to the ground you get, the more they jiggle. Fast shutter needed! And don't you press the lens up against a window, either -- unless you like blur. Maybe more than any other type, aerial photography is about *sharpness*.

Film supply? Your time over target will be limited. If you will use a 35mm, load 36-exp cartridges, and they should be full. If you have two camera bodies, load them both. Who wants to be reloading, when you need to be shooting?

What lens? Either a normal or a mild wide angle. My favorite is a 35mm wide. Needless to say, you won't need to worry about focus -- everything will be at "infinity." Think about sharpness instead.

Some of the big boys use a larger format camera for aerial, for one reason: More detail. Unless you already have a large format camera, I do not advocate you rushing out to get (or borrow) one for tomorrow's aerial gig -- you won't be familiar with it. A 35 you know is better than a 4x5 you don't. Digital? Don't even bother.

And another interesting fact -- the best work is done with the plane's window down, and the door off its hinges. That means there's nothing between your lens and the target but air, nice cold air, whipping by your face at 125 knots and more. HEY! I'M FREEZING!

It's cold up there. Now you know why pilots get to wear those nice fleecy jackets. Gloves too. And, oh yes, *cameras* can freeze up there, too. I remember a Pentax that locked, a Rolleiflex that froze so tight in seconds that it buckled a shutter blade, a Leica that stopped, and a Speed Graphic that slowed way down... Are your cameras up to the cold?

So prepare. Study. Find out where it is, and what it is. What SHOULD it look like from the air, and what are you supposed to get? Look at other peoples' work. Make sure you have working equipment, and discuss your needs and intentions with your pilot, before you take off.

Preparation pays off. Good luck!

SKIN ART

Once you're taking pictures of people, you'll soon find some of them come with interesting ornamentation -- and a lot of that ornamentation is very photogenic. Whether you want to do a spot of fashion photography, or just close-ups of tattoos and piercings, there are some things you need to know -- a lot of things, in fact. Let's cover a few now.

We need to talk about **color temperature**. In the old days, when things were black-and-white or not at all, all you needed from the light was that it be more or less white and that there be enough of it. Still true, for black and white. But we're not Puritans, we don't wear dark, somber, boring clothes (do *you?*), and as they say, "tattooed folks are colored people." Who needs black and white? Let's talk about *color*.

The sun, daylight, has a particular "color temperature." Yes, I know its *hot*, out in the summer sun, but *color temperature* really means *balance of the spectrum* -- what percentage cool blue, what percentage warm red, etc. A "warmer" light has more yellow and red, and a "cooler" one is heavier on the blues and greens. You need to know this.

You see, most color films are "balanced" for daylight. That means they give "true" colors under the bluish light of the sun, of electronic flash, or of old blue-tinted flashbulbs. If you use them under incandescent light, everything will be far too yellow-red, because incandescent light has *higher color temperature*. You've seen those horribly yellow-orange "available-light" attempts with "daylight" film? That's why. And of course fluorescent light is different from either of them...

There are two things you can do about it -- you can use filters on the camera, or you can use a film that is corrected for incandescent light instead. If you use filters, you need to know they cost you a lot of light! Suppose you have ASA 100 film, and can take your shot at 1/50th at f2.8. With the correcting filter in place, you'll likely need 1/25 at f2. Use of a filter forces you to use faster lenses, wider openings, and slower shutter speeds. Sometimes there's not enough light, when you're using a filter.

If you're using slide film (far more precise than color negative) you can get "type A" or "type B" films formulated for incandescent light -- but mind using these films outdoors -- in sunlight, without the proper orange filter, they'll make everything very very blue.

If you're using C41 film (color negative), it is all nominally balanced for daylight -- there are almost no commercially-available incandescent-light types. They'll tell you your over-yellow images can be "color-corrected" at printing time, but *for a fee, by a skilled printer.* That means a "pro-lab," or custom-processing, *which means a large stack o' dinero....* If you use Wal-Mart's processing (pretty good, most of the time) or Snapfish, or any of a few other cheapies, *there won't be* a skilled operator correcting your colors -- and they'll be yellow. *Yeah, and you wanted to show a nice, colorful tattoo.....*

So what do you do about it? THe best light source for skin art? It's the *sun*, folks. A nice bright day... Otherwise, you *will* need to color-correct.

You already know (I've mentioned it) that **zoom lenses are not all that sharp**. I don't care that your 28-300mm wonderspecial do-it-all has a "macro" setting! It's *NOT GOOD ENOUGH*. Got that?

I've seen, and photographed, some of the most intricate, delicate, fine-edged work ever inked onto a human being (Debra Valentine's work comes to mind), and tattoos that fine, that sharp deserve photos al least as fine and sharp. Zoom lenses, especially in low light, cannot deliver a sharp enough image. They just *can't* -- and I don't care what the salesman says -- his job is to move the goodies, not to tell you the truth (and remember, if it looks like trash, they'll blame *you* -- the jerk who took the pictures -- and odds are you'll fall for it...) Truly sharp close-up work is accomplished either with the traditional "normal" lens, or with a real "macro," a specialized lens optimized for maximum focus at ranges under 3 feet. These will provide shots *at least twice as sharp* as you could get with any "macro-zoom" lens. You need that sharpness.

An aside about photographing fresh tattoos. Tats are a bit red when they're fresh. The best photos come a few hours, or a few days, later. A healed tattoo, covered with a bit of clear massage oil, photographs well. A *new* one, ten minutes after you put the needle down, will be raised, red, somewhat inflamed looking, and won't be quite as nice to look at. If you can wait, best to do so. Otherwise, what about taking one shot now, and another in a few days?

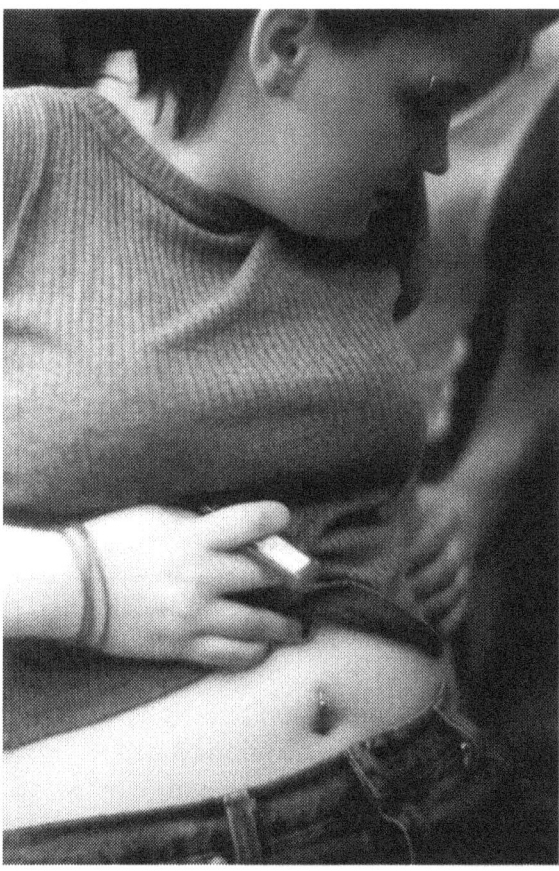

What about piercings? Most new piercings will have stainless steel jewelry in them. Of course the light needs to allow the skin tones to photograph as they are -- and the silver color of the steel. Again, sunlight is best -- either outdoors (though sometimes you *can't*, without risking a visit from the vice squad) -- or a nice north-facing window. You'll need sharpness. I can't imagine anything dumber-looking than an out-of-focus shot of a piercing. The picture should be as sharp as the piercer's needle.

Again, like tats, piercings look better after they've healed, after the swelling has had time to go down. Most people don't have the time to wait for it -- but if you do, it will look better.

Some folks will want to take pictures of tattoos and piercings with a flash camera. You certainly solve the color-temperature problem that way -- but it causes other problems. Unless you have a TTL Flashgun, a *real* one, one that *uses the camera's inboard light-meter to control the flash's intensity and duration*, you run the risk of too much light. Most flashguns, even TTL types, do a trashy job at close range. And, because it's a flash, you won't know whether it'll be all uneven and glarey until you see the finished photos. That's chancy, especially if dollars are on the line! Stay away from flash unless you have to use it, and unless your camera has true TTL, don't use it at all for tattoo photography -- you'd be firing in the dark.

Lighting is a complex subject. You can spend thousands on good lights, and the studio portrait photogs *do*. They don't need this book -- you do. You do need to think about "hot spots," though. A "hot spot" is an area of uneven lighting that causes a glare highlight. As tattooed skin is often oiled, to make the colors look better, hot spots are a risk. They occur because more light is falling on one area of the picture than another -- they are a sign of uneven lighting.

All the things I've said about tattoo photography and close-up work on piercings apply to fashion photography, which I define as consistent and deliberate concentration on people's costumes. That includes the tats and piercings, along with clothes, hair, footgear, and whatever else contributes to the decor. Suppose you're doing hair? same things go as with a tattoo -- but where a tat comes with its readymade background (your *hide*), hair sticks up there, and you'll need to show some concern with background. If you're covering a show, make sure you choose a non-distracting angle. If you're shooting "on location," choose backgrounds that contribute to the mood you're trying to set (alleys, beachfront, outdoor ice cream parlors, etc.) PLAN your "fashion" shots!

Planning is the difference. Where one shooter just gets a "hot new camera," and says "now *I* can do "professional work," the serious photog has the right camera, the right film, the right lens for the job, and knows, from the beginning, what the "right" pictures will be. That's the discipline of photography, and it's just as true for skin art as it would be true for photos of rocks, butterflies, or medical study materials.

WAR PHOTOGRAPHY

In his excellent *Hazardous Duty*, Dave Hackworth tells the story of a fresh-faced, cocky young J-school photog grad, who showed up in Vietnam, ready to take his cameras into battle. He was very very sure of himself.

"First, lose that yellow baseball cap," Col. Hackworth told the boy, "It makes you a target for snipers."

The neophyte wouldn't listen. "We shipped his body home on the next plane," writes Col. Hackworth.

There's a moral: *If you find yourself in battle, never for one moment think you are beyond the reach of its consequences.* The purpose of war is to kill people and break things, and it's a safe bet at least one side in the conflict you wish to photograph considers you a fair target. And they're not kidding. You may not be "subject to military discipline," but I strongly suggest you act as if you were. Listen to the commander -- and follow his instructions. You'll live longer.

What's a good war photo? Good question. What are you doing there? Who are you working for? Are you there to show "our side vs. their side? To borrow a concept from the sciences, what is your "research design?" *A "research design" is first a statement of your hypothesis, and then an enumeration of just how you plan to go about proving or disproving it.*

You can't photograph everything -- and you need to decide what kinds of images to look for, before you start. Seriously.

Suppose "it's not your war." Suppose you're at the scene of a conflict that has nothing to do with you, for which your country is officially neutral. Do you understand the issues? From BOTH sides? These people are killing each other -- do you comprehend why? And, do you comprehend why they might not wish to have your cameras pointed at them?

You'd better.

My point: Nothing's simple. If you're going to go cover a battle zone, you'll do a better job if you understand the issues before you get there. Read up. Listen to BBC (*they* still know what "value-free reportage" is, even if American media have all forgotten), and then go find a few nationals, a few citizens of the country, and interview them. It'll help.

How much do you know about war? Are you one of those folks who calls every long gun an "assault rifle," because you heard it on NBC? Get over it. *Get yourself informed.* I know, *you think "My job is to take pictures," but you need to know what you're looking at!* What kind of aircraft? What kind of tanks? Who is supplying them? You'll do a better job when you know. You NEED to know. In WWII, American correspondents (and many GIs) called every German Tank a "Tiger" -- and most *weren't.* Get your facts right.

And one more ethical issue: The battlefield is no place for a pacifist, or a Quaker. You may well be put in a position where you may have to fight, to *kill,* if you would survive. Can you pull a trigger, to save your life? If not, don't go there.

War is the ultimate test of ruggedness and reliability. Men who are not at the highest level of fitness -- will be defeated. Equipment that is long on features and short on brute reliability -- will break. This holds true for both weapons and cameras. Nikons got their reputation in Viet Nam, where, under filthy, wet, tropical conditions, they kept running, and brought home the pictures. You'll need cameras that are super-reliable, can take a battering, and are simple to use. Anything extraneous -- will break, just when you need it.

There are a few obvious considerations, like: Where are your pictures going? Do you have a market? Do you have a particular editor advising you, before you go? Otherwise, stay home. Don't be an idiot.

In most other aspects, war photography is just another version of "dangerous service," and what I said there will apply. If you're going, remember *the gringo with the cameras is always a target*, and take care of yourself.

SMALL OBJECTS

"Museum Photography? Archaeology? Small Objects? Why? That's *boring...*"

You might think so. Some of the happiest days of my life were when I spent nine months photographing every object in a museum, one at a time. I fell madly in love with the curator, a classy lady with bright red hair, and I got to spend 8 hours a day alone with her, taking pictures of chipped flints, little pots, and other ancient objects. Sadly, nothing came of the romance, but the pictures are still there...

What about taking pictures of small objects? I've already told you a lot (The principles don't vary; only their application) but there's always time for a review:

Depth of field: You know that's the distance on either side of the focus target (farther and nearer) that's in acceptable focus. You know the closer you get, the smaller (in inches or millimetres) is this zone. You also know that the more wide open the lens (as in low light), the smaller the zone. Now, think about a close-up, taken under bad light. Yep, you got it! No depth of field at all! And if you're wiggling too, that picture's gonna stink.

Cure: Have a workspace with some floodlights. Have a lot of floodlights. It's like being "too rich" or "too thin" -- there's no such thing as "too much light" for a close-up. Remember, as you stop down, adjusting for all that plentiful light, you increase the depth of field... And, use a tripod!

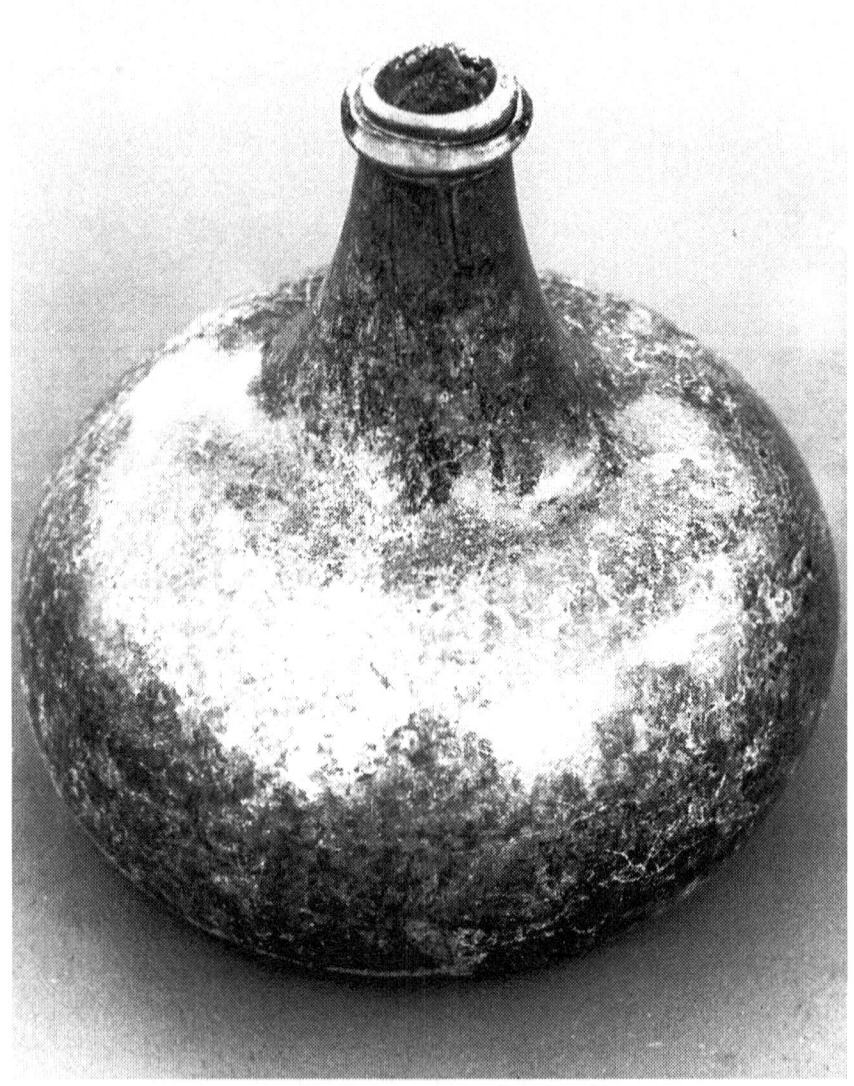

Mark your rolls, so you can tell them apart. Maybe frame I should be of a "title-board?" After you've shot umpteen hundred little flint arrowheads, they can all begin to run together in your nightmares -- and you don't want to put the wrong picture in the wrong file, do you?

What kind of photos are you taking? B&W, Color Slide, Color Print? Digital (I hope not!). Elsewhere, we've covered how digital just isn't very sharp. Added to that, your museum work needs to be "archival," it needs to endure for a long time, and electronic storage media is NOT archival. Color slides are pretty archival, or should be, if stored well. There will still be an image there in 50 years... But, the color of the slides, especially those processed 25 years ago in cut-rate houses, may well change. Your artifact slides could look like artifacts themselves!

Archivally-processed B&W lasts the longest -- but poorly-processed B&W can go off in two or three years. Like rotten fruit, poorly-processed photos give off chemicals that can damage the good ones stored nearby. They go brown, and, when it's bad, you can smell them. I've been in "photo storage galleries" that weren't going to survive long enough to allow the dig to be written up. A lot of archaeological images CANNOT BE DUPLICATED -- so get it right the first time.

Backgrounds: A lot of small object work will be (or should be!) shot against a plain cloth background of appropriate color. Take a fragment of painted pottery. A black and white shot, under the same lights, at the same distance, can look strikingly different with a black vs a white background! Black velveteen has a way of "disappearing" in the print, leaving that creamer, or chamber pot, suspended in space. It's useful.

With color photography, have a few cloths of different colors, and try a color complimentary to that of the object. The appropriately-colored background'll make a difference.

I've harped enough at you about sharpness and good processing. With museum work, remember that the collection of photos is a catalog of the collection of objects. The photos don't matter for themselves -- they are tools to help the researcher better understand the objects themselves -- so you'd best be orderly, consistent, and accurate in your preparation of the photo collection. It's NOT AN ART -- any more than is being an aircraft mechanic.

Last and most, as an archaeological/museological photographer you're most likely working for someone else. How much time have you spent with this person? Spend more. You need to know what your boss wants, and how your boss thinks. Your job isn't to wow anybody, or to be creative in new and unique ways, but to be reliable and consistent. You're not an artist; you're part of a research team.

WEDDING PHOTOGRAPHY

A wedding is a symphony. There is a structure to it; a flow, and any decently informed person can predict the high points -- and the order in which they will occur.

But no two symphonies are alike, and, you're not there listening/observing; you're a *participant*. You have to catch it, as it happens.

Now the symphony orchestra has a conductor, and the wedding action follows the priest/celebrant's lead, yes, but a lot *just happens around him*. You have to be ready. It's like those old parlor games where, at a given point in the music, the rubber bear is going to jump up, you *know* he's going to jump up and roar, and then you have to shoot him with your popgun, but you aren't sure *exactly* when -- and *you don't want to miss that bear*. You'd feel pretty stupid if you did.

Photographing weddings is like that.

Unless the wedding is in *your* church, and you've gone to a lot of them -- get your butt to the rehearsal! Walk through the "dry run" with the couple and their priest. Ask them what they're doing that's unique. Talk to the parents, the Best Man, the Maid of Honor (this is when they can also tell you what *they* want, so *you* can get it for them -- and just incidentally make *more money*). It's called "being ready."

Do you know the order they'll follow? Have you figured out where you'll have to stand? Have you checked the light, the backgrounds, and whether or not you'll need to use flash for everything? *I don't like flash. Some churches require it -- but others are so beautiful as they are, a flash feels like apostasy.*

Are you clear on the processions in and out? You don't want to be like the pricey, swank young photog I observed who, laden with equipment, moved like an arthritic nonegenarian, and managed somehow to be *behind* the new couple as they emerged from the church. Shame on you, guy.

A marriage isn't just a "marriage." Its also a gathering of relatives, young and old. Be fast, and get shots of the children and oldsters. Look for interesting and amusing moments; don't just snap the predictables. You're molding memories for the next century -- don't let them down!

Equipment? Here's my choice. I carry a number of bodies. In a big, open church, where there's no restriction on my movements, I may line up 5, 6, 7 Nikons, all loaded with the same ASA 400 Fujicolor (**don't mix film speeds!**) and just go. My flash cameras will be TTL-equipped Nikons with dedicated Nikon SB lights. If you're going to flash in enclosed spaces, and do people, true TTL (where the camera modulates duration and intensity of the light during the exposure) is worlds ahead of anything else. My favorite cameras, in such circumstances, are the FA and the old N2000 -- which has all the features you need in a light package. Lens choice depends on where I have to stand -- and will range from the 50mm fl.2 to the 35mm f2 and 85mm fl.8.

What about a quieter, more traditional (read: "no flashguns") wedding, with enough light? Get your meter readings during the rehearsal. For these I use my Canon 7 rangefinders (a lovely, almost forgotten competitor to the Leica M3) with the 85mm f2, 35mm and 50mm fl.8s. They're quiet, un-ostentatious, and mount good sharp Canon glass. I'm a big fan of using rangefinder cameras in low light.

Every wedding features "lineup" shots. Do them *outside* -- if at all possible, without flash. Here, SHARPNESS! For these, I keep a Leicaflex SL with 35mm Elmarit f2.8 (a slow but brilliant lens) that has never let me down. You'll sell lots of prints from a lineup -- so treat it with *respect*. And, listen to what folks are asking for -- they're the hand that feeds you. Don't bite.

Film budget? My average, for wedding plus reception, is eight to 12 rolls of 24 exposures each. Carry more -- and take ENOUGH pictures. Like a musician playing an encore, you're there to make THEM happy. Don't shut your instrument off til it's done.

Pricing? Here there is leeway. The traditional "photographic McDonalds" treatment *(here comes another one, just like the other one...)* was to shoot 12 or 15 "set pieces" and sell a package. Easy to do, but where's the LIFE? Where's the UNIQUENESS? They missed it. They could offer a "package" price because they knew before they went what they'd have when it was over. *Like a robot wedding....*

I don't work that way. I charge a fee to show up and shoot. It covers my film and processing -- and not much more (Are you paying too much for film and processing? Probably). To make significant money, I have to be "with it," and I have to get goodies that will sell. I have to sweat. So what? That's life.

Then I take orders and sell the prints *a'la carte*.

VISUAL ANTHROPOLOGY

Visual Anthropology ("visual ethnography") sounds complicated. It isn't. It sounds mysterious, "academic," highbrow, out-of-your-reach. It isn't. It's just good, careful documentary photography done with a few important caveats, and ALL documentary photography could benefit from its lessons. *I speak of **good** visual ethnography, of course -- there's plenty of the other stuff out there, and all one can learn from it is "don't go there."*

A prime purpose of anthropology is to teach members of one culture about the ways of another culture; "Social Studies." Photography has been an important tool for as long as anthropology has existed; the two disciplines literally co-evolved. A great deal of surviving early photography, once we get out from under the influence of dreary, uninspired 19-th century portrait/landscape painters, is anthropological in charecther (and thus of high use to the anthropological historian.) But is it good visual ethnography?

The old images, like archaeological treasure troves, are full of data, lost sights we will never encounter again. For that, we can, and should, use them. The people who took them "were there," were/are *witnesses*. But we should not consider them "expert" witnesses! We ask of good visual ethnography that it reflect a balanced viewpoint, and that it not overly manipulate the subject. We ask that it be more "honest," less self-centeredly judgemental, than the travelogue snapshot collection. The old photographers, in general, do not pass this test. "A biased witness is better than no witness," if he had a camera in his hand -- *but **only** if we remember he was a **biased** witness!*

Just as there are two types of "traditional" written ethnography: holistic and process, the same two divisions can be applied to visual work. An ideal visual essay on a group, a tribe, a society, is an evenhanded depiction of all aspects of their life, free from negative (or overly positive!) judgementalism. Is this 100% achievable? Of course not -- but like "the sin-free-life," the impossibility of achieving perfection should be a spur toward greater effort -- not toward the morally relativistic, "anything goes" PC of our current crop of Marx-worshipping "Post-Modernists."

You'll never be "perfect;" now do the absolute best you can.

A "process" ethnography, visual or traditional, deals not with the whole of a society, but with a single issue, such as folk music, funeral rituals, children's games, or the behavior of men in combat. Other than that, traditional rules against falsehood, omission, judgementalism, and propagandisation apply. As with "holistic" treatments, perfection is unattainable; one simply strives to do *the best possible job.*

The Hiesenberg Effect

German physicist Hiesenberg stated that the presence of an observer, and the act of recording an event, inexorably changes that event. It sounds pretty esoteric, and can lead to acey-spacey casuistry about whether anyone hears when the tree falls, but in the field of social science, Hiesenberg has some validity -- as it does in photography. Is it a fixed constant, the Hiesenberg Effect? Of course not.

Consider two photographers. One clunks into view, with piles of cameras, tripods, equipment, "attitude," the latest "Pho-togs" brand-name approved *I'm-in-J-School-and-I'm-somebody* clothing, and jams his huge camera in your face, forcing you to make him the center of your reality for the moment, to react to **him**. The other is very understated.

The second photographer does not come across as a self-important "other." She speaks the local language/dialect, does not use her clothing to differentiate herself from her subjects, engages them in meaningful conversation before and while getting her images, treats them as her equals, and allows them to teach her about themselves. She gets better pictures than her egocentric *artiste* of a competitor.

Photographer #2 *will* modify her subject reality by her presence and her work -- but *far less* than will photographer #1. As long as she does not pretend her presence changed *nothing* (and as long as we, the viewers, don't either) her work is better visual ethnography than his is. He is perhaps an excellent advertising, commercial, or fashion photographer -- but she is sticking to ethnography's game plan -- reporting about, describing, a culture. He isn't. He's using it to make, not its points, but *his own*.

Two factors set these two photographers' approaches apart. Assuming they are of equal ability (and many fine photographers would be miserably bad ethnographers), the first difference is in *goal*. Photographer #1's goals were something other than to learn and explain the subject population to the readers. He may sell more pictures, and tittilate a wider audience -- but the dollar sign is not the measure of ethnographic quality.

Her pictures may lack "mass appeal," but ethnographers will be able to feel reasonably secure in using them. HER images will inform subsequent generations. His will wrap fish.

PHOTOGRAPHY AND YOUR CHILD

Photography is too much fun to leave your children out -- and besides, children haven't learned to "hide behind words" the way we have -- so their very way of seeing is different, and can produce some incredible images. You can learn from your kids. Plus, show me a parent who doesn't want their kid following in their footsteps? And, a karate *sensei* told me once that *the best way to learn something is to have to teach it.*

For a kid, photography isn't about cameras; it's about *seeing.* Talk to your kid about *the moment.* Teach them about the image that "gets it," whether it is the dog licking someone's face, the cat jumping out the window, the magic look on your friend's mom's face when she wins the turkey raffle, or the bull on the hilltop silhouetted in the orange sunset.

There is time enough for them to learn the darker, more depressing imagery of "adult" photography -- and, you never know, they might never choose to go there. *Peter Pan with a camera -- there is no "truant officer" coming for you if you stay a child...*

A child needs some basic training. Teach them about "good light." Teach them to hold still, and not ruin film by "limp-wristing." Teach them not to spray film like a frightened machinegunner.

Take your child's age into account, and keep the camera inexpensive. By age 13, a child may be ready for an old SLR and external, hand-held light meter; younger kids need to think about images, not equipment. Digital? I wouldn't; film cameras teach *patience*, and no one progresses in photography without this, the rarest of all virtues.

Most children, and their parents, share a few major failings: They need to get closer to the subject, and they need to recognize the moment. Take your kid with you on a few shoots? A day at the racetrack, or the amusement park, can provide lots of instructive situations. You should get some good ones too. And, I've never met a kid who wasn't uplifted by "doing what daddy does." Ever.

Have standards (about blur, bad framing, too-far-away, and wastage), but do not expect your child's pictures to look like yours. There are plenty of different ways to see.

Some of the points I bring up here may seem "old-fashioned," but isn't that what parents are for? To pass on the wisdom of their own generation to the next? We are far too in love with the *Avant-Garde*, with "newness" for its' own sake -- and our children will learn the new without our help; our job is to preserve what we learned -- by passing it on to them. *Teach your children well...* and be prepared to learn from them.

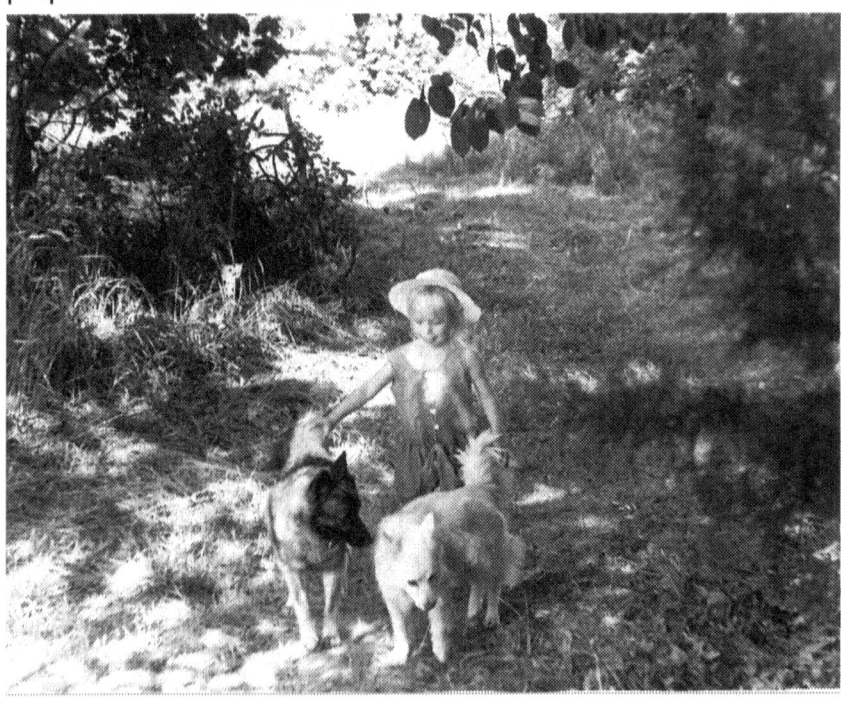

EDITING

"PICTURES OF THE YEAR" is an annual photo contest held in Columbia Missouri. Editors choose from the year's most memorable news pictures, and post those they judge to have the best impact. As "If it bleeds, it leads" is an icon of American journalism, the choices are usually dark, dismal, depressing, and familiar. This is not a "photography" contest, in any artistic sense of the word, nor is it a search for creativity. Just blood. Blood, death, misery -- the things we love so much. Right.

One particular picture, at the 2002 POY contest, aptly illustrates the perils of photo editing. It is from Afghanistan, and in it, three Northern Alliance fighters are shooting to death a prisoner from the Taliban. The guns are firing, and spatters of blood are flying from his body as the bullets strike. It is unquestionably a photo of the act of murder.

However, we mustn't let the most obvious blind us to the rest of the evidence. If you look closely at the prisoner, you see circumstantial evidence of a second atrocity. The man is dying as the shutter snapped, yes, but his pants are down around his ankles, and soaked with blood -- far more blood than has had time to come out of the bullet wounds being inflicted upon his body at that moment. He bled, profusely, before he was shot!

Why? I suggest his tormentors emasculated him. Got a better explanation?

Now, they did display the photo; so what did they do wrong? They *ignored the obvious*. One of two things happened: Either they did not pick up the evidence in front of them -- which calls their competence as photo editors into question, or else they did, but chose to say nothing -- which feels like *bias*, from here.

Now, let's talk about photo editing.

When I was a kid, I remember reading about *Black Star*, which was, and still is, one of the world's great photo agencies. Its boss, Howard Chapnick, had a column in *Popular Photography*, and I read every word, eagerly. I remember, in one issue, how he followed a photoessay several of his people had done in China. This was the 1970's, so it was one of the first.

The photographers took perhaps 40,000 pictures, and edited the collection down to about 2000. Chapnick himself edited their material down to about 400, and sent it on to the customer, who, I believe, used six. This, said Chapnick, was typical.

When I was doing my apprenticeship, I asked one of the photographers I went out with what his "use rate" was. He said "one in nine." That's a bit better than one in 5000 -- but the same message holds -- every shot isn't going to be just what the customer ordered.

What *did* the customer order? Who are you working for? What are you doing there? Most pictures are paid for by someone who decides, in advance, what they want. Have you talked with this person? Do you understand what they want? Do you *agree* with them? Can you translate their wishes into images?

Only a small percentage of photography is "pure" news, and many would say with the bias in today's newsrooms, and the wholesale promotion of "the news" as a product, as something to sell, the news is hardly "pure" anymore.

Most photography is "commercial," that is, it is done in service of a paying client. Most photo editing consists of weeding-out those images contrary, or not directly congruent with, the wishes of that paying client. *Therefore it pays you to know what those wishes are.* Do you?

Most editing is subtractive; it consists of *taking things out*, of making a collection smaller. What deserves to be eliminated? Once you eliminate the poor exposures, poor printing, obvious technical snafus, and images blatantly off the point, what's left is a matter of opinion. A second judge will probably have a different opinion. *It's like a poetry contest.*

How do you edit your own work? Before you pick up the camera, you know what you're there for. Then, once you've gotten your images, and you've eliminated all the garbage, all the stuff you feel the need to apologise for, look for the duplications. Pick the best. Don't expect to do the final editing -- that's for your employer to do -- but you can trim down the mass before you pass it on.

If and when you edit other people's work, be sure what you and your employers want. Be sure you see everything in the picture, not just that which is most obvious. People aren't stupid -- and they'll see what you miss. The best thing is to not miss it.

Remember, editing is not a science, it is an art.

ARCHIVAL STORAGE

So you have a collection of pictures, and you intend to keep them more than a few weeks. They're your stock-in-trade, the source of your income. They are your livelihood. What do you do? Bung the lot into a shoebox? Scribble pertinent info onto the back of each?

Nope. The three sides to photography are sufficient *planning and preparation*, good *technical execution*, and optimum *storage and retrieval*.

First, lets talk about "archival" *storage*, which means *maximizing image permanence*. How long should your pictures last? What's reasonable?

Given half a chance (good paper, stable ink, good storage conditions) the printed word can last 500 years. I have personally examined books printed before the Spanish Armada sailed, in the time of Queen Elizabeth I. Their parchment pages are chemically stable, and their lampblack ink is inert. Lovingly cared for in private libraries, these volumes have outlasted time -- and there is no reason to believe they won't last *another* 500 years.

But while traditional text printing is, or can be, inert and stable, photography is a chemical cocktail. With good processing and enormous luck, traditional "fiber-base" prints might last 100 years. The newer, more convenient "RC" papers are probably not as stable. Color prints are still less, and thirty-year-old slides are often so faded and color-shifted as to be useless.

What do you do? Years ago, when I worked for Star Photo, a huge regional processor in Madison, Wisconsin, an instructor told us that color photographic emulsions were like fruit. "When they're too fresh, they're green," he said. "When they're ripe, the colors are brilliant, and, when one 'goes off,' it shifts toward the purple." Just like rotten fruit.

To further the useful analogy, "one bad apple spoils the barrel." Rotten fruit gives off noxious gases, and these accelerate spoilage amongst any fruit (green, ripe, or overripe) within reach. One poorly processed print or set of negatives, engaged in the remarkably similar process of "going off," gives off noxious gases that accelerate spoilage in its neighbors. And, in color print materials that are too old (well past sell-by-date,) poorly processed/stored (under too hot conditions) or otherwise failing? Purple -- just like rotten fruit.

Useful tidbit: Process them right the first time, then they won't kill their neighbors in protest. (*Sounds kind'a Marxist, doesn't it? But, this is chemistry, not humanity...*)

How shall you store finished images? Assuming you've done your best in processing -- with fresh chemicals, sufficient time in the fixer, and adequate washing -- where shall you store them?

Not in your darkroom! Prints, negatives, and slides are intensely vulnerable to corrosive gases. The stench coming off an inadequately-processed print (we've said) can destroy its neighbors, but even more the gases and suspended particles given off by in-use processing chemicals. By definition, a darkroom is a place full of chemicals that can damage the permanence of photographic materials -- so store your finished products somewhere else.

Just as with fruit, excessive temperature can accelerate "going off." Unprocessed film and paper are enormously unstable, of course, and should be refrigerated to retard spoilage. No need to refrigerate processed images, but "room temperature" (20 c/68 f) and a reasonable humidity (30 to 50%) are ideal.

In what will you store them? Some containers give off the same corrosive gases you've been trying to avoid. If you use plastic sleeves, know there are two types. Some are made of polyvinyl chloride (PVC) and others are made of polyvinyl acetate (PVA). PVC is cheaper -- but gives off corrosive gases that can in time degrade the very images you were trying to preserve. PVA is stable, and it is the material of choice for photo storage.

Some cardboard boxes and manila folders are assembled with glues that contain corrosives. Rubber cement contains gasoline! You don't want your pictures in these containers. There are stable glues that do not degrade photo images, and "acid free papers" (the same ones that do not quickly fade like a cheap paperback book) for envelopes, boxes, and blotter pages. Ask at a good, established photo store -- not at some joint in the mall where some high-school refugee will try to sell you a digital camera.

Digital storage: A CD-Rom is pretty secure. Problem: We're not talking 5 years, we're talking 100 years, and in 100 years, that CD-Rom, and the computer to read it, will be worse than artifacts -- they'll be landfill. There is absolutely no reason to believe the JPG and TIFF formats, the CD-Rom, the Windows and Mac operating systems, and the programs you use to create and view the images will not be replaced, superseded, and forgotten. What good are your digital archives then?

There's nothing wrong with scanning in your prints, cleaning them up in programs like *Adobe Photoshop* (I do it) and burning them onto CD-Roms. It's a good idea. Back up your data often. But -- it is **short-term** storage, not **long-term**, that you're doing. *Remember, a few years ago, when a couple of recording engineers wanted to do a "digital re-master" of one old Beatles album, they discovered it was cut in 3-track(!), had one hell of a time even finding a 3-track machine at all, and had to do strange and wonderful things just to get it to play the tape, once, so they could make a "modern" copy. And that was how many years ago?*

Electronic technology changes too fast to be considered a viable long term archival storage option.

Next question: How do you propose to find them again? How do you find that picture of the 1939 Bentley you took in Hungerford, England, in 1987? In my case, I use digital formats for retrieval. I scan the prints in to hard drive, at at least 350 dpi (sharp enough to please most publishers), and save them in multiple categories: "Old Cars," "British Portfolio," "Presentation," etc. I create categories meaningful to my work -- and you should do the same.

Pictures I have previously sold migrate to a folder called SOLD -- as many publishers do not accept previously published work.

Doing this, scanning in my "keepers," allows me the convenience of digital to solve the problems of retrieval -- while keeping my paper masters in good archival storage. As some publishers buy digitals, I can sell right off my hard drive. Note: This is possible because my scans are at sufficient resolution. Don't clog up your hard drive with 100 dpi scans you can't do anything with! THERE IS NO WAY TO RAISE THE "DPI" NUMBER, ONCE AN IMAGE HAS BEEN SCANNED -- DO IT RIGHT THE FIRST TIME.

This issue, storage and retrieval, is not thrilling, but once you have 10 years' worth of images, or 20, and you take a good look at them, you'll almost certainly find some moneymakers in there. They are your "stock file," and a good bit of your income can come from selling them -- but only if they remain in marketable condition.

Get it right.

YOUR PORTFOLIO

What goes in a portfolio? Every photographer has one; what shall you put in yours? To say "your best work" is not informative, and we need to give the matter some thought.

What is the purpose of a portfolio? *It has only one: To persuade the viewer to hire you.* It is not properly a narrative, and less is it an autobiography. Like a salesman's display case, it is merely a collection of your wares. What do you have to offer?

Some people sell out of their portfolio. If you're going to do that, remember you're selling *images*; you're not selling *yourself*. You're selling the products of your skill and experience, not the STORY of how you got there. Your customers are *not* buying the story of your life -- they're buying images they find attractive. Remember "meaning is observer-applied," and your customers will be seeking images that resonate with their *own* meanings -- not *yours*. Avoid captions. Want to tell "your story?" Write an autobiography.

Any piece of work you feel the need to "explain" -- should not be there. Any piece of work not representative of your present capabilities -- should not be there. Even more, anything you feel the need to apologize for -- should be removed. The portfolio is a selling tool, not a retrospective, and unless you can deliver something like *that one,* **now**, what's *that one* doing in there?

Maybe you're looking for employment? Your portfolio should show prospective employers what you can do for them. "Past successes" should only be included as proof of your present abilities and experience. Make sure to "tune" such a "job portfolio" to the needs of the employer -- do NOT load it down with images impertinent to the job description.

How big should your portfolio be? Absolutely no more than fifty images. Once I built my first one, and reached my fifty, ever after, when I produced another image I thought was "portfolio quality," I went in and pulled out the weakest one in the portfolio, and replaced it with the new one. *It's amazing what problems you find in pictures you chose for your portfolio last year! "How could I have put THAT in there?"*

A portfolio should be always updated, always reflecting your best. Good work you did 20 years ago can and should stay -- if it measures up to the best you're doing now -- but only if. And again, if you have to explain it, you shouldn't include it.

A portfolio is not a stock file. Your stock file is the indexed collection of all your potentially marketable images (hundreds or thousands!) and you're unlikely (I hope) to haul the lot out for anyone but your photo sales agent. There is no limit on the size of your stock file -- it is your "sales warehouse."

Think of your portfolio as an advertisement. What do you want to advertise? Keep it short, keep it powerful, keep it pertinent, and remember you're not advertising *yourself*, but your *wares*. Put yourself in the buyer's (or employer's) shoes, and prune everything that is off the point. *For a different buyer, or a different employer, load a different portfolio, and make it pertinent to their needs and wants.*

What's in mine?

I like pictures that "sit up and bark." As I wrote in my gallery-book, *Outerloper*, I prefer amusing pictures, ones that show the familiar in a new light, bringing a smile, a jolt of *bel canto* familiarity, or a giggle, to the viewer. There's a tiny baby sitting on a horse, almost lost under a ten-gallon hat, a frog approaching a sign that reads "Pride," an ancient "Flying Service" sign on a tall tower, now fallen to the ground, a shot of the US Womens' Olympic Rowing Team, taken from directly above their boat -- and they look like a gigantic water-strider, a single, wind-blown English poppy in a field of green barley, even a moody morning shot of Dublin's "Halfpenny Bridge."

What's *not* here? Death, destruction, chaos, pain, war... I think some folks are sure only "darkness" sells, and, to "be competitive," each one feels the need to find something more horrifying, more depressing, than his fellows. Yuck. I'll shoot such pictures, on assignment, but I sure won't put them in my portfolio!

Again, there's no reason you can't have several portfolios, each pertinent to a given situation (I have one strictly for horses!) or even "pack" a portfolio for a specific interview. What's in your stock file? If it's a "fashion" job you're applying for, better make sure the images in there are all of people! If it's a "sports" job, show 'em what you can do with the theme. No pretty houses or mountain scenics.

Displaying your portfolio

The traditional portfolio is a big zipper case with plastic sheets. It is expensive, fragile, and the sheets yellow with age. It may also, I suspect, be damaging to the archival stability of your photographs -- so you'd better ask. If you have to "show" a lot, it may not be very practical, but "portfolio-viewing" is a tradition-laden act, and you really need to follow the norms. *An unusual, "wacky" way to present your pictures, just like a purple CV, is probably not a very good idea.*

Some people may ask for a portfolio on CD-ROM. If you know what you're doing, and are comfortable with digital imaging, take some copies with you, but don't assume people want it, or would be comfortable with it. If they think you're trying to show how "hip" you are, trying to show you're "more with it" than they are -- you'll probably lose the sale. *If you have a good digital portfolio, you might ask, before the interview, if it would be appropriate?* Don't make an issue if it *isn't*. And of course if your digital abilities aren't up to snuff, if you have to apologize for the images, that's just as bad as including substandard work in your physical portfolio. Don't go there.

Hopefully, I'll get a look at yours, someday...

PHOTOGRAPHY AS A BUSINESS

Maybe you'll be hired somewhere, as a photographer, and paid a salary. Most of us aren't so lucky (and remember, the copyright for work done on salary belongs to the salary-payer, not the employee), but most of us have to *sell our pictures, shot by shot and job by job*, to eat.

Like rock and roll, photography is a "reputation" business. People pay more for the big names. Partly that's because of "investor" buyers -- the kind that buy art (and photography) so they can resell it at a profit later, and partly it's because the big names are, as a rule, more 'reliable,' and, hiring them, one can be assured they'll get it right the first time. But you're just beginning.

Are you reliable? Can you deliver a good product the first time? **Business comes before art**. These people have some reason for wanting a professional to do the work -- or else they'd do it themselves. Are you "professional" enough? "We don't want excuses; we want pictures!" said one editor to me, years ago. You've presented yourself as a "professional;" can you back it up?

Most consumers of professional photography are not there to buy art. They need either journalistic depictions of a moment: News, sports, press-releases, public relations... or a visual presentation of their product, to accompany their latest ad campaign. They want a skilled craftsman, not an *artiste*.

Then there is the matter of **guarantee**. Most of the time, you'll be paid when you produce what the customer wants, and not before. You may like the shot -- but if they don't, tough. *Customer satisfaction.* That's the way it is.

So what can you charge? What is the "going rate?" What will "the market bear?" Remember the folks with the most-established reputation in that market can charge the highest. Starting out, even if your work is great, you'll have to charge less -- if you care to feed yourself. The phrase "priced himself right out of the market" needs to be remembered.

In some cases, you'll find out the going rate is lower than what you'd like, perhaps lower than you can afford. Tough. Cut your costs, and live with it, or else find another market. Business is like Newtonian physics -- things are as they are, whether you like it or not.

Have you looked at your costs? Do you know what is the cheapest source for film, processing, and supplies? And don't get huffy -- nobody cares if you're paying more to "buy American," or if you're buying "green." They want their picture at *that rate*, and if you *can't deliver at that rate*, they'll get it somewhere else, from someone who *can*.

Regarding reshoots: You'll have noticed most money-back guarantees don't offer the option of a redo. Big business has so many clients they don't mind losing one -- and they figure a redo ain't worth the time. **You can't do that.** You need, unless the customer is unpleasable, and demands it, to offer re-shoots. "Cash upon satisfaction" is a good policy. It keeps the customer happy, and happy customers come back for more. Guarantee money back, but offer re-shoots. That way when there is a botch (and there will be, trust me), you don't lose that client. And learn from your failures.

You might find yourself in position to create a new niche market. Your particular blend of skills and interests might put you where there is demand, but no competition -- but remember, markets don't stay secret, and as soon as you build a market, others will try to horn in on it. Even if you have no competitors at this moment, keep your prices down and your quality up. Then, when some brand new upstart arrives, and wants to challenge you for market share, you'll have the best advantage there is -- reputation.

A PHOTOGRAPHER'S SOCIAL SKILLS

If you're going to make your living photographing anything more than trees or inert objects, you'd better be able to get along with people. Even if your favorite subject is stamps, coins, or flint arrowheads, it pays to know how to relate with strangers -- especially the ones who sign your paychecks. Here are some hints:

1. Nobody likes an *artiste*. You're not being paid to be creative -- you're being paid to put form and shape to your employer's vision. You're a craftsman, not an architect.

2. Good work is invisible. It's not about *you* -- the best work makes you think of the product -- not the photographer. Keep your ego out of your work.

3. Know who you're working for, and behave appropriately. You're not so precious that you can't be replaced, if you come across as a *jerk*. So be respectful. If you can't, find another sport.

4. Do some homework. Have some idea of the situation, and, if possible, of what has been done before. Not only will it save time, but it helps ensure you don't come across like a total rube -- which can affect your reputation, your job security, and the size of your fee.

5. Your human subjects are neither props nor extras. Show them some respect; they'll talk about you. You don't need them

spreading negativity -- and what they think of you really *does* matter.

6.   Keep your promises. Before you promise delivery of work -- THINK. Can you deliver it by that date? Better to add a few days, rather than failing your own deadline. A slow promise *kept* beats a fast one *broken*, 8 days a week.

7.   Be patient with your employer. Graphical reasoning is your business; you have no difficulty generating an appropriate image to fulfill a particular theme. If your employer had the same ability, he'd not need *your* services! Photography is your business -- not *his*. Help him realize his needs. He's not a moron because he has difficulty explaining them to you.

8.   What about the people around you? You are NOT the most important thing in their lives; try to be unobtrusive. Please. If they want an actor playing the part of a hotshot photographer, they'll call up central casting and hire one -- and he'll be better looking than you are. Get over it.

9.   Be prepared to go the extra mile. This is a "reputation" business. Folks who see you work harder and deliver more than expected -- will ask you back (and happily pay to have you there.)

10. Be aware of local customs. One of the fastest ways to get blackballed is by embarrassing everyone. If you're in an unfamiliar place, you might want to ask about specific local "ways" that might interfere with photography. You WON'T come across as "weak" for asking; but as humble and considerate -- good virtues, those.

11. Above all, be flexible. In an art studio, you'd have control over events. Outside, on the street, you are observing reality -- and reality is unpredictable. Be prepared to follow where reality leads. One of my editors had been a surfer boy, from California. He said that following a breaking news story was like *riding a surfboard.* "If you stop to look down at your feet, you'll wipe out."

He's right. Keep your eyes on the goal, bend with the waves, and get there.

LITTLE STORIES SECTION

A KID PHOTOGRAPHER GETS LUCKY

By the time I was fifteen years old, I was crazy about photography. I'd done my first work for pay two years before, and I read all kinds of books about photography and photographers. I fantasized a lot, of course. Of course, being a teen, I was convinced I already knew everything...

I had a photo club. I was president, of course. We'd just had a meeting, and most of my friends had gone home. My friend Scott was still there.

Scott's family were firemen. I think he grew up in the firehouse. Like the firemen, Scott had a pocket pager that sounded whenever there was an alarm.

It went off. So did the neighborhood hooters.

Scott called in, and the department told him where the fire was. He came back to me, very excited.

"Get your cameras," he yelled, "It's Hilltop School!" (He and I had "done years of time" in the place, and we remembered it well, though without much fondness. The prospect of seeing the place in flames was both exciting and satisfying.)

I grabbed my Leica, and we got on our bicycles. I don't think we'd ever made the trip so fast.

When we arrived, there was steam and smoke coming out of the boiler room. Fire trucks were everywhere. Sure of myself, I got my camera ready, and went right into the burning room.

First thing I saw (mind, this was a hot summer night) was an old fireman, in his rubber suit, with his helmet off, wiping his face. He looked overheated, and, as steam was everywhere, I wasn't surprised. I readied my camera.

As I tripped the shutter, he collapsed. I got a picture of him half way to the floor. Heart attack. He died right there.

Fellow firemen came running, and I got out of the place.

Now I'd read that when you have something special, you should seek out an editor you trust -- but I didn't know any editors. There was a local weekly, and they might just be interested. My mother drove me down the next day.

It was a bit scary. I left them my film, and got out of there.

My friend Scott called me the next morning. He had three words for me: "Front page center."

I went back down to the paper.

The editor wanted to see me.

He was a huge grey-haired bear of a man with a wooden leg. There was a battered 4"x 5" Graflex on a shelf behind his desk.

He had the picture. He had a check for me. He asked me if I wanted to *really* learn photography?

Of course I did.

He'd been an Army photographer, a compatriot of Joe Rosenthal, and he'd been on Iwo Jima, where the Japs shot off one of his legs.

He still missed news photography, but, unable to get around very fast, he'd "moved upstairs," buying a weekly, becoming an editor.

He saw something in me. I was terrified I'd disappoint him.

Maybe I didn't. If I did, he was enough the teacher to keep it hidden, and keep me going forward.

He talked to me about the 1940s, when he'd been a combat photographer, but more the 1930s, when he was learning the business -- when he'd been a kid like me. He introduced me to the work that had moved him -- the images that came out of Roy Stryker's FSA, the U.S. Government photo unit that first employed Lange Evans, Mydans, Delano, Lee, Rothstein, Post Woolcott and more. I think I was as knocked over as he had been, way back when the images were current.

He instilled in me a deep respect for the old ways and the old ideals, and he taught me that modern "automatic" machines, however they may improve "convenience," are no more improved tools to great art than a computer synth to a symphony orchestra.

The most we can do today, with our automatic autofocus digital Chinese computerised whizbangs is, if we're lucky, maybe duplicate a few images first recorded 3/4 of a century ago, by people using hand-made, manually-adjusted machines just as sharp, just as capable of producing profound images as are our "latest model" super-cameras. Take one off the shelf; a Leica, a Contax, a Super Ikonta, an old Rollei, a Speed Graphic; see for yourself how far we haven't come since.

This man saw past my teenage belligerence and attitude. He may not have taught me all the tricks of the trade (who ever knows them *all?*) but he passed me as many as I could master.

He sent me out on assignments, and, in spite of the lessons, he paid me for the images I brought back. I'll never forget them.

One evening, he assigned me to photograph a city council meeting, on the eve of a local election. Remember, I was 15 years old. He told me not to mind they were older, or "officials," or even the age difference. He told me I'd be surprised how biddable politicians get when the media is present!

"Move them around," he said. "Tell them what you want them to do -- they'll do it."

I was astonished. Order adults around? He meant it.

That was also the time he gave me a real gem; he taught me to get the "bread and butter" shots done before I started to get cute. He said it was better to have a good, sharp, boring shot, than a bunch of chance-takers that didn't work out. "Call it insurance," he said. "Then you can take your riskier shots; if they work, that's great. If they fail, you still have the "bread and butter" safe in the camera."

He sent me to cover local art fairs, sports events, a fire department turkey raffle (I won a big turkey, too, and had the devil's own time getting the bird home -- was my mother ever surprised!); one of the earliest public television fundraisers, a program where local young people appeared as extras in summer opera productions, and more.

The day after freak tornadoes had pulverized the area, killing dozens, secure in my job, I went right into one of the collapsed buildings (seven had died in there) and brought back photos. "Let's see what you have for me," was all he asked when I brought him a stack of prints.

I'd worked a 12-hour day, covering damage in the neighborhood. He gave me a 33-photo feature spread. As he paid by the shot, I made some real money that week.

I worked for the old man, and learned from him, for two years, and my debt to him is incalculable. I hope, when I'm as old, gray, and irascible, to find some wet-behind-the-ears youngster, and pass it on.

But, there's one lesson that really sticks with me most. In one of the books he assigned me to read, the writer, a young news photog, had gotten lucky the day before, and, like me, had a front page center photo. But it was the next day, and he was bragging.

"Did you see my photo yesterday? Wasn't it sharp?"

"Sonny, they're wrapping fish in it today!"

MY STRANGEST ASSIGNMENT

When professional photographers meet, they swap stories. One of them, frequently amusing, always instructive, is "my strangest assignment." Listen to a few of them, and you realize how nutty life can get! I know of one photographer, who had to photograph a new Mercedes, as a *blur*. Just the right length of blur, and just the right background, of course -- but a blur.

He did it -- and they gave him the car, as payment!

I know of another, who had to shoot an ad for a hotel chain, and for some godforsaken reason, the Art Director (the one who dreams up the ad images, and hires/fires photographers)had decided he should have a shot of the company's president/CEO -- in the bathtub -- with a rubber duck.

The CEO was not particularly cooperative.

But *my* strangest assignment was a bit different.

It sounded simple enough. It was a karate *dojo*, and they were having "promotions." I was to do several group shots, then a single portrait of each student who passed his/her examination. There would be a total of more than 60 pictures -- so I should do pretty well.

So I thought -- til I got there.

The *Sensei* (who called himself, somewhat grandiloquently, *Shihan Dai*, "Grand Master"), explained to me that every "promotee" would have to break at least one concrete block. "Like this!" he demonstrated, slapping one with his forehead, and raining rubble in all directions. "I want you to get every one of them in the act of breaking their concrete."

Uh-huh. And no re-do's, right? Probably break my head... Oh well.

To avoid battery failure, I plugged in my strobe. I was prefocused, and had answered all my exposure questions. The only thing left to chance was timing.

Like many firearms, the Pentax (what I was using at the time) has a two-stage release. This means the shutter button travel continues down to a stop, and any further pressure will release the shutter. As each "promotee" took his position before his concrete "victim,"

I squeezed the shutter until I felt that second stage, and held there, til he bellowed out his *"kiai"* yell, and smashed his blocks.

Would you believe, the pictures were pretty good? I think the most advanced student broke eight or nine blocks at once. I got a great one of a brown belt breaking six at once, with his head. It looked like the World Trade Center, with his forehead mashing it down...

I don't think I missed any, but there were a few "balks" by less-than-fully prepared students. I got pictures of these students NOT breaking their targets. One of them was an overcocky brown belt, who, bloodied by his failed attempt, swung again with his injured hand, and broke his blocks, bloodily, on the second try. *Bushido.*

The sensei ended the event by breaking 9 blocks at once with his knee, which had just had arthroscopic surgery. He walked away from that one fine.

What an evening. I think I was more exhausted than the students, but I had the shots.

READING PICTURES: A CASE STUDY

When I was ten or 11 years old, I was crazy about cars. This wasn't unusual, I don't think. I learned names, appearance, country and city of origin, and, above all, dates, for a lot of types, brands and marques surely no one has mentioned since.

I was a genuine junior-sized automotive bore. Really.

Now at just the same time, my school bought into a new, and newly-published, series of Geography books. I remember lots of photos of the earth taken from outer space, lots of fancy maps that made the continents look like a peeled banana, and all those pictures taken of the wide, empty thoroughfares of foreign cities.

Those city pictures (Bangkok, Manila, Tirana, Istanbul, Athens...) really bothered me. They were all black-and-white, and diminutive, and they all had the same credit-line: "Photo by Ewing Galloway."

I'll never forget the name.

Now things were pretty jingoistic back then, and the fact so many cities were portrayed as "empty" didn't surprise me -- after all, these places were *POOR!* Albania? C'mon now.

What bothered me was the *cars.*

Remember, this was the 1960s, and these books, fourth, fifth, and sixth grade geography texts, were *newly published.* In all these photos, the cars I could see were ancient -- consistently ancient.

Now would it be surprising to find that in Ankara or Tirana some people drove old cars? No. What bothered me was the cars were *all* 1930s machines in *all* the photos of *all* the foreign cities (all taken by Ewing Galloway) -- *and newer cars were not visible.* I remember asking my teacher about the oversupply of old machines in Manila, Istanbul, Madrid, Athens, and Bangkok. "That's how it is, there," she replied.

Rubbish.

It took me 20 years to get the answer. If an item relates to the practice of photography, I'm going to try to read it. I think it's a good idea. I was reading about photo agencies and stock sales agencies, and there was *that* name: *Ewing Galloway.*

He did his work in the 1930s.

I'd been right. This geography book series, assembled in the 1960s, had been illustrated with selections from a pre-WW II stock file. As these were not pictures of archaeological sites, famous people, great art, or antiquities, but purportedly of the metropolitan capitals of the world, this was a serious failure.

And one eleven-year-old caught it.

THE ASPIRING JOURNALIST

(This one also appeared in my anthology *Raindancers*, published 2003 by 1stBooks/Authorhouse.)

He was about 20, recently married, with a head full of dreams. He didn't have very much, and hadn't done very much, but he read incessantly, and, as much as book-learning matters, he did know something about his profession.

He wanted to be a newsman, a photojournalist. He always had a camera, and bored his friends and acquaintances to tears with it. But it was always loaded, always ready.

He was headed home, one afternoon, from god knows what, down the main street toward the apartment, when he heard a commotion from across the street; men yelling.

Then a gun, a big revolver, came sliding across the pavement, stopping only inches away from his feet. A running man, a cop, breathless, followed right behind it, scooped up the weapon, and dashed toward a bus, which was just pulling away from the stop.

There were suddenly half a dozen cops, surrounding the bus, beating on it with their pistols, screaming.

Up came the young man's camera.

The bus stopped, the door opened, and the cops charged in.

What was going on?

In a moment, they emerged, dragging a black man of about 30. They pulled him off the bus and threw him against the side of a building, where they commenced to beat him, with fists, nightsticks and gun butts.

The camera did not stop.

Then the police saw the photographer. One called out, and ran toward him. The young man ran.

He figured the cops would beat him too...

Nearby was a funny little store, run by a man from China. It sold restaurant supplies to the many Asian food stores in the city, and its back room was full of huge bags of rice, noodles, and beans with unpronounceable names. He slipped inside, as if a customer, headed for the back room, and ducked out of sight.

About half an hour later, he used the store's pay-phone to call the "City-Desk" Editor of the local paper, and tell them what he had.

"Wait right there," said the City Desk Editor. "I'll ring back."

Where could he go? Like he was going to go out on the street now?

The call came. "I called the police, and asked them what happened. They told me; and I can't use your pictures."

"Why not?"

"It seems the man was in a bar, drinking, and shooting off his mouth. He said he'd like to 'kill a cop.' An off-duty cop was listening, and called for backup."

"Yes, and they beat him up."

"But there was no gun. So, no story."

"Are you saying that...?"

"Yes. If he'd had a gun, I'd want your pictures. Since he didn't, there's no story. I can't use them."

Censorship? Of course. Turn a blind eye to gratuitous police brutality? Of course. *"See no evil!"* Were the cops white, and the victim black? Of course.

Things were different, back in 1974.....

IN CONCLUSION

What are you doing there? Why do you have a camera in your hand?

Some of you will answer: "It's part of my job." Your employment requires prepartion/maintenance of a visual record -- **and you're doing exactly that**. OK.

Some of you will be doing simple documentary: "This is how it was, right there, right then. Your pictures are, will be, an important part of the historical record. They are a *mirror of the truth.*

But is that all? Is a photograph just "a mirror," albeit a highly selective one? There are many excellent photographers, folks whose work I respect, who believe so. If they encounter ugly, depressing truth -- their pictures will be duly ugly and depressing. Their photographs are indeed **transcriptions of the truth**.

I believe there must be more.

Can one batter the viewer with sufficient visual unpleasantness to guarantee the desired change? *Of course that such behavior makes you a propagandist indeed must go unsaid.* Too often, the torrent of suffering simply causes sensory overload. People tune out; they become hardened to the suffering of others. They become, not surprisingly, jaded.

I believe that life is beautiful. Despite our materialism, despite our bad attitude toward each other and the world we live in, despite our best efforts, life is mysterious, extreme, passionate, sometimes harsh, even stark, but always beautiful.

A few photographers epitomize this: Brassai and Cartier-Bresson, Duncan, Stieglitz, Steichen, Ansel Adams, Roman Vishniac, the FSA team, the exhibitors at *Family of Man*, Hugo Van Lawick, Rod Brindamour, even Oskar Barnack himself. Above all, I'd place the "lyrical documentary" of Walker Evans. His idea, that there can be a transcendent beauty in the simple and mundane, is a treasure for us all.

Hugo Van Lawick, whose pictures turned his wife, chimpanzee researcher Jane Goodall, into an international celebrity, wrote that the photographer (most specifically the *nature* photographer) has a duty to inspire, to uplift. I agree.

We are, or should be, more than historians, more than journalists, more than documentors of a past instant. For our readers, *our images,* I believe, *must be proof of the possible, must inspire folks to do better.*

That's how I see our job, our purpose.

P.J. Nebergall

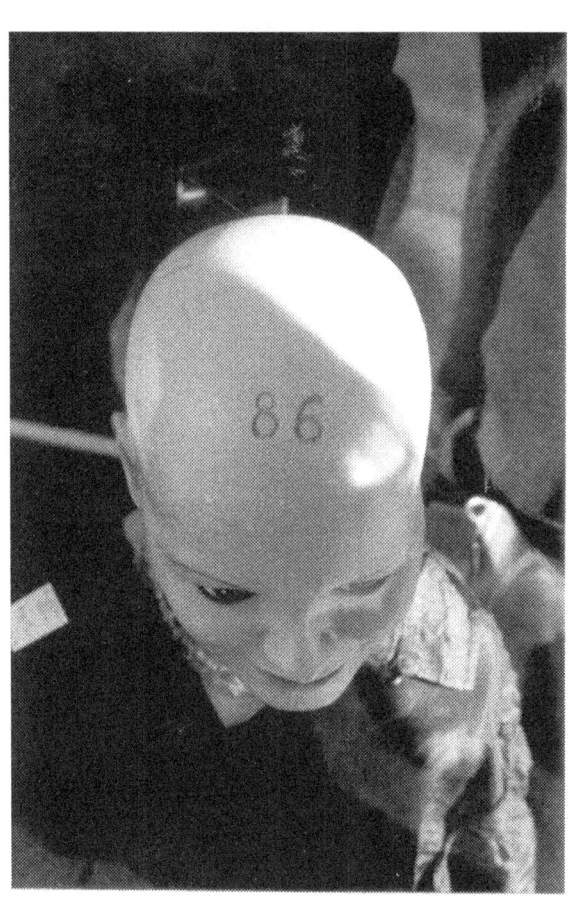

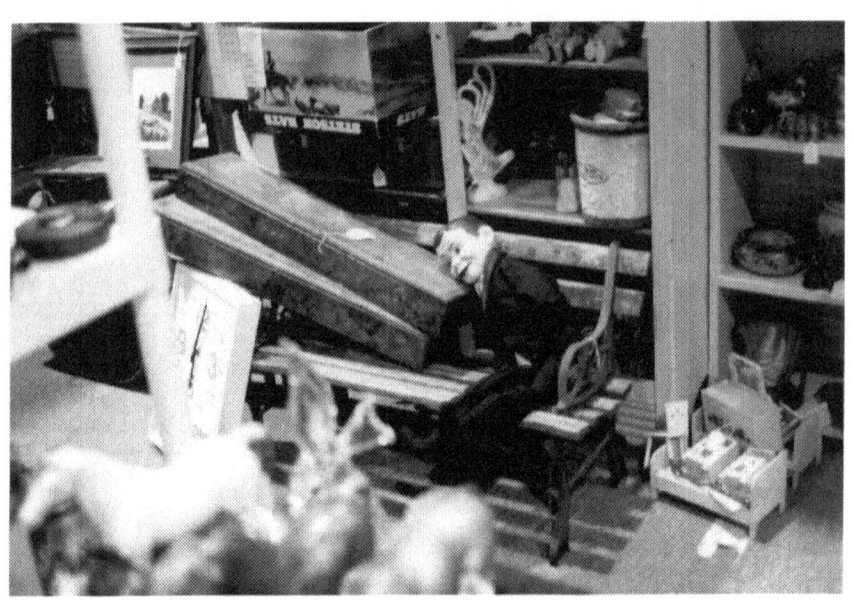

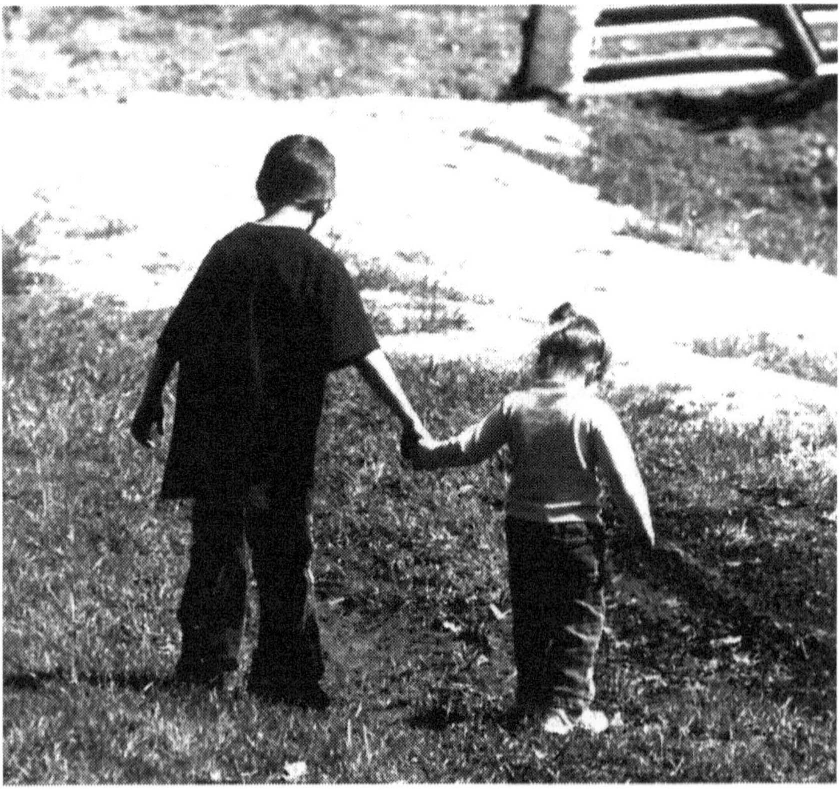

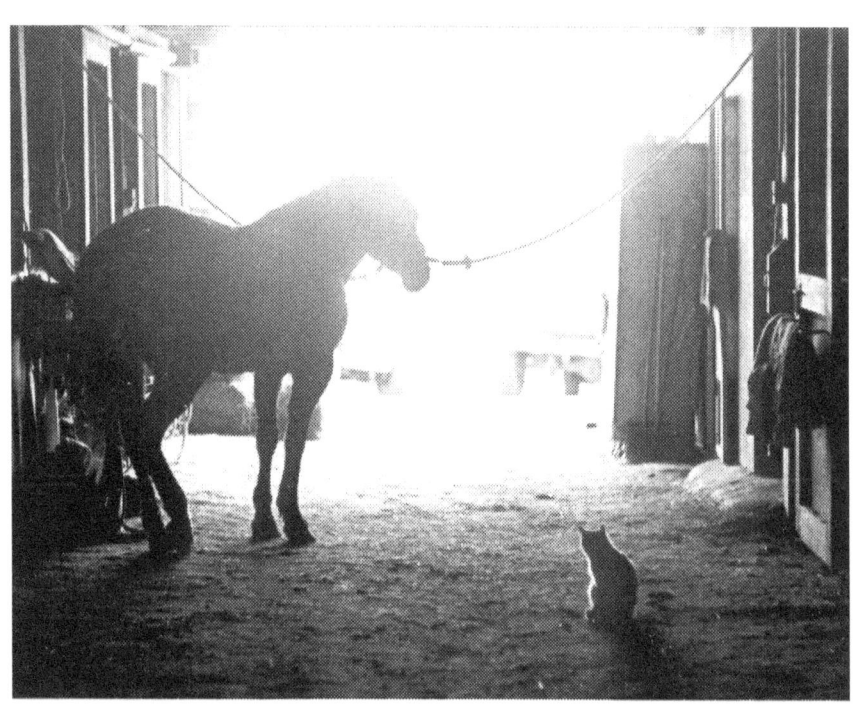

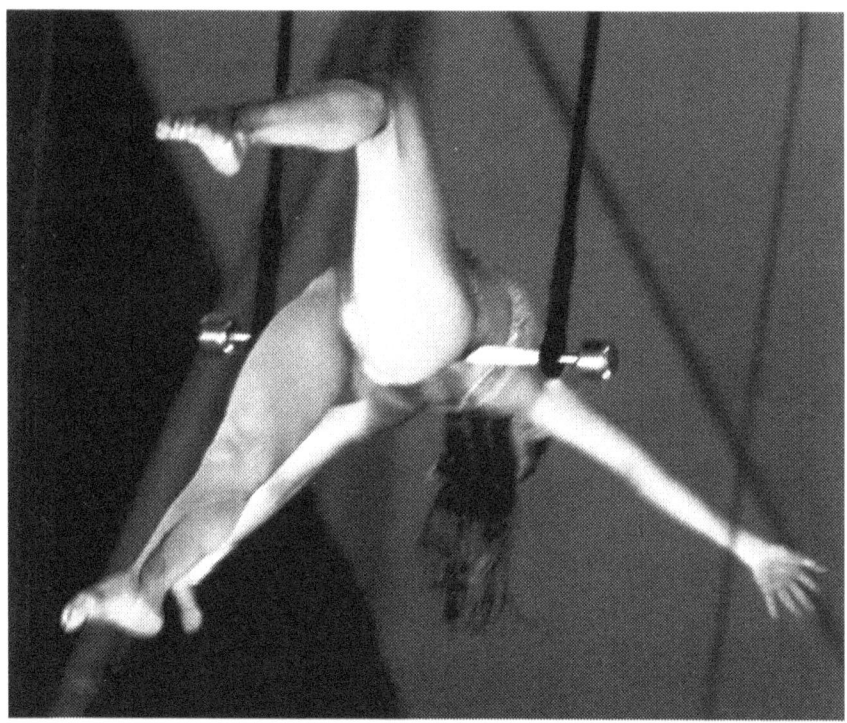

APPENDIX: Reading List

Most of these photographers produced many more works than those named here. The list is by no means exhaustive. I include these as "starters," because I have personally found them valuable learning tools. Start here, and go on...

Adams, Ansel
  Ansel Adams (edited by Barry Pritzker)
  Crescent Books, 1991
Atget, Eugene
  Atget's Paris
  Taschen, 2001
Brady, Matthew
  Matthew Brady (edited by Barry Pritzker)
  Crescent Books, 1992
Brassai (Gyula Halasz)
  The Monograph
  Bulfinch Press/Little, Brown & Co., 2000
  Paris by Night
  Pantheon, 1987 (reprint of 1933 edition)
Buchheim, Lothar-Gunter
  U-Boat War
  Knopf, 1978
Burrows, Larry
  Vietnam
  Knopf, 2002

Curtis, Edward S.
  Edward S. Curtis (edited by Barry Pritzker)
  Crescent Books, 1993
Duncan, David Douglas
  Yankee Nomad
  Holt, Rinehart, and Winston, 1967
Evans, Walker
  Walker Evans
  MOMA, NY, 1971
McCullin, Don
  Sleeping With Ghosts
  Aperture, 1996
Magubane, Peter
  Vanishing Cultures of South Africa
  Rizzoli, 1998
Nebergall, Peter
  Hard Core: Marginalized By Choice
  Loompanics, 1997
  Faces of Punk
  Xlibris, 2003
Riefenstahl, Leni
  Five Lives
  Taschen, 2000
Riis, Jacob
  How The Other Half Lives
  Dover, 1971
Stieglitz, Alfred
  Alfred Stieglitz (edited by Eva Weber)
  Crescent Books (1994)
Thesiger, Wilfred
  A Vanished World
  Norton, 2001
Turnley, David and Peter
  Moments of Revolution: Eastern Europe
  Stewart, Tabori, and Chang, 1990
Van Lawick, Hugo
  Among Predators and Prey

Sierra Club Books, 1986
Wagenvoord, James
Hangin' Out: City Kids, City Games
Lippincott, 1974

Collections:

America at the Crossroads: Great Photographs from the Thirties
(FSA, edited by Jerome Prescott)
Smithmark 1995
Bound For Glory: America in Color, 1939-1943
(FSA/OWI, edited by Paul Hendrickson)
Abrams/Library of Congress, 2004
Explorations: Great Moments Of Discovery
(The Royal Geographical Society)
Scriptum, 1997
The Family of Man
(MOMA, edited by Edward Steichen)
Simon and Schuster, 1955
Flash! The Associate Press Covers the World
(edited by Alabasio, Tunney, and Zoeller)
Associated Press/Abrams, 1998
The History Of Photography
Beaumont Newhall
MOMA, New York, 1988
100 Best Vintage Photographs
National Geographic Magazine, 2004
Picturing Modernity
The San Francisco Museum of Modern Art, 1998